Parenting for a Peaceful Home

Parenting for a Peaceful Home

Challenges and Solutions for Almost Perfect Parenting

edited by
Louise K. Horvath

CATHEDRAL PUBLISHING
Pittsburgh, Pennsylvania

Published by Cathedral Publishing, Pittsburgh, PA 15260
Copyright ©1997 Cathedral Publishing
All rights reserved
http://www.pitt.edu/~ondemand
Manufactured in the United States of America
Printed on acid-free paper
Design: Kathy Boykowycz
ISBN: 1-887969-04-7

Parenting for a peaceful home : challenges and solutions for almost
    perfect parenting / edited by Louise K. Horvath.
    p.   cm.
    ISBN 1-887969-04-7 (alk. paper)
    1. Parenting—United States. 2. Parent and child—United States.
3. Child rearing—United States. 4. Child psychology—United States.
5. Interpersonal communication—United States.
I. Horvath, Louise K.
HQ755.8.P3792   1997
649'. 1—dc21   97-36483
                                               CIP

Contents

III. Living with Older Children

IV. Management and Discipline for a Peaceful Home

Acknowledgements

This book was compiled with the input, assistance, and guidance of the following staff professionals of the Parent & Child Guidance Center: Joan Lanz, Lois Greenberg, Jane Blair, Carmen Marcano-Davis, Sheila Griffin, Iris Harlan, Wendy Levin-Shaw, Alice Mahler, Richard Seiler, Irene Surmik, Rod Willaman, Jill Wolter, and Karen Wien.

Parent & Child Guidance Center

Parent & Child Guidance Center is a nonprofit agency offering mental health and mental retardation services to children, families, and individuals in the greater Pittsburgh area. The Center's mission is to provide the opportunity for the healthy growth and development of families. For more than 40 years, the Center has offered parenting education to parents, professionals, and other caregivers in order to enhance their effectiveness in raising children. The Center's popular parenting seminars form the basis for this book.

About the Editor

Louise K. Horvath is the public relations director at Parent & Child Guidance Center. She is a former teacher. Ms. Horvath has long used her public relations and educational background to promote the welfare of children and families. She wrote the radio series for which this book is the companion text.

Introduction

Raising a family is rewarding, but it is never easy — especially in today's fast-paced world. Two-career families, stepfamilies, single-parent families and even traditional two-parent, single-career families face challenges unheard of by their counterparts in previous eras. Today's parents yearn to be effective — to provide the framework in which their children can grow into happy, productive individuals. But it seems they're frustrated at every turn by obstacles ranging from too little time to increasing media influence.

Most parents could use a little help now and then in creating a peaceful home — the kind of environment in which families flourish — and that's where this book comes in. Rather than a step-by-step instruction manual, this book acts as a "coaching guide" for good parents who want to be better. It's for parents who are looking for effective communication skills and problem-solving strategies that can help their families thrive.

Everyone has his or her own ideas about "good parenting." You may not agree with everything in this book — and that's okay. You're the parent and you can choose what's best for your child from the options presented. The book's practical suggestions for meeting your family's challenges represent the combined expertise of seasoned professionals and provide an overview of the issues modern families face. None of these suggestions should be taken as absolutes. It's up to each family to choose what works best for them.

We suggest you begin by reading the first chapter, which includes key issues facing parents of children of any age. Next, you may wish to read the fourth chapter on general issues of discipline, since it also applies to children of any stage of development. Then scan the table of contents for chapters that apply to your child's age group. From the last chapter in the book, you can pick specific topics on personal development for parents that may apply to your family.

Keep this book handy as a reference the next time you need a little parenting help; then pull it out and read a pertinent chapter. Whether you read **Parenting for a Peaceful Home** as a whole or on an "as-needed" basis, we hope it will help you, not just once, but many times in many different ways.

1

Foundations of Parenting

1. Families today
Challenges of parenting in the new millennium

The American family has undergone an evolution, of sorts, in the past few decades. Families today are influenced by a variety of social forces. Understanding these trends can better prepare parents to raise their children in this fast-changing environment.

The changing role of women has profoundly affected families. As more women enter the workforce for personal and economic reasons, the balance of parenting has shifted. With both parents working, many fathers have become more involved in raising their children. Families are more dependent on outside child care, teachers, and youth leaders to help their children develop. As a result, many children are finding other adults to serve as mentors to complement their parent's role. The community is becoming involved in a child's growth.

Families now experience more divorce, separation, and remarriage than before, creating new challenges for stepparents and blended families. At the same time, it's important to ensure that children gain the love and commitment they need from the prominent adults in their lives.

With more than half of children under five years of age living in single-parent households, parenting alone has become another significant challenge. At a time when extended families are a rarity, single parents must learn to make use of friends and community leaders to help their children develop into responsible, caring adults. Single parents often carry the full burden of economic support, emotional care and motivation for their children, leaving them feeling isolated and pressured.

The issues confronting stepfamilies often are complex. Almost every stepfamily experiences grief from the first dissolved marriage. Parents may have completed the healing process, but the children often have not. Some kids won't let go of the fantasy of reconciliation. When a parent remarries, the fantasy is destroyed. The matter is further complicated when the second marriage also fails (between 67 percent and 80 percent do). The multiplicity of relationships that some children must endure is frequently overwhelming. When parents explore the reasons why their previous relationships failed, they can gain a better understanding of themselves, which can benefit the welfare of the children in blended families.

Children today have much more freedom, opportunities and advantages in the family. For example, smaller families mean that many kids have less responsibility to care for siblings. This may mean they have more time to participate in activities, such as soccer or band. But children also have greater pressures within, and outside of, the family.

The high school used to be the place for the rite of passage from childhood to adulthood. It was a place where adolescents could try out adult behaviors — even negative ones — in a safe environment, where there were adults to protect them. The growing use of drugs and alcohol forces many kids to confront adult issues at an early age. Sexually transmitted diseases and teenage pregnancies are also on the rise. Suicide rates amongst teens are at an all-time high. These truly are troubling times.

Families coping with our rapidly-changing culture need to stay in close communication with each other, offering a secure environment in which growth and love take place. This book will help parents and children get started and stay on the right track to building a successful family.

PARENTING POINTERS

➤ American families are coping with a number of trends today, including the changing role of women and the growing competition of outside activities for families' time and attention.

➤ Stepfamilies and single-parent families are meeting the challenge and creating new models of cooperative, supportive family life.

Efforts need to be made in these situations to understand children's feelings about change.

➤ Parents need to acknowledge the benefits and risks to their children of today's atmosphere of increased opportunities, activities and pressures on kids to succeed.

➤ Communication is the key to maintaining a safe, caring, and loving family atmosphere.

2. The parent-child relationship
How to know if you're on the right track

Most parents want nothing more than to have a good, long-term, and positive relationship with their children. Such a relationship can provide a great deal of joy to both parent and child. However, this requires parental commitment, infinite patience, and respect for the child as an individual and an important member of the family.

Parents can find it helpful to examine how their parent-child relationship is faring. Doing this can help parents learn new ways to improve the bonds with their children. What signs should parents look for to indicate a healthy relationship or one that may be showing signs of problems?

The primary sign of a good parent-child relationship is how well the child is functioning in the world and contributing to life at home. The parent-child relationship is affected by the personalities of the parent and child, the child's age and stage of development, and the parent's overt and implied expectations. For example, a parent who is very outgoing would be wise not to judge his relationship by whether his introverted child communicates profusely with him. To develop a good relationship it's important for parents to have confidence in themselves and in their child's ability to reach his or her fullest potential. Research has shown that children sense this confidence in their abilities and respond positively.

In a healthy relationship, the key message that parents convey to their children is that they will always be there for them, and that no matter what they do, the parent will always help them make it right. An example of this is when a teenager may need to feel free to call her parents to rescue her from a drinking situation. She needs to know that even though she was somewhere she shouldn't have been, her parents will come and get her and be understanding.

On the other hand, what are the signs that a parent-child relationship may have problems? If a parent finds herself continually angry with a child, and if small problems seem to become big issues frequently, the relationship may need to be examined more closely. Or, the parent may find himself talking to the child in a sarcastic, lecturing, or insulting way. Frequent spankings or excessive discipline may also indicate trouble with the critical bond between parent and child.

If upon reflection the relationship seems unhealthy, parents can take steps to change things. First, after quizzing themselves about how realistic their own expectations have been considering the child's personality and stage of development, they can talk to their child about his or her observations and brainstorm about solutions. This alone may improve things. Or, the parent can focus on some small areas for success — perhaps better communication during the dinner hour — which can set the ball rolling and lead to other interactions. Another step is to expand the parenting repertoire, by reading a book or attending a parenting lecture. However, if the unhealthy relationship doesn't improve and seems to be interfering with the child's functioning at home or school, seeking professional help may be the answer.

The important thing is that parents look closely at his relationships with their children and work on the necessary adjustments. One way to do this is to discuss with each other the specific events during the day. Consider the positive and negative effects they might have had on the relationship. This helps the parent start looking, thinking, and understanding about how to improve this critical parent-child bond.

PARENTING POINTERS
➤ In a good parent-child relationship the child will freely express herself to the parent and willingly spend time with the parent.

➤ In an unhealthy parent-child relationship the parent may find himself often yelling or disciplining the child.

➤ Frequent reflections on the parent-child relationship can help parents identify areas for improvement.

3. Self-esteem
Recognizing and enhancing a child's self-image

Most parents understand how important it is to help their child develop a positive self-image. Self-esteem is a key to future success. When a child feels good about herself, she can do just about anything. To evaluate a child's self-esteem, parents can ask themselves questions about several areas of their child's life.

First, parents can look at their child's interactions with others and sense of ease with himself. Does the child feel comfortable in his clothes, with his own body? Does he relate to people in a positive way? Is he a member in good standing of the family and with friends? Answering "yes" to any of these questions indicates self-esteem in the making.

When a child feels unique and confident, she possesses a good self-image. To assess this, a parent might ask, Does the child feel prized and special? Is she able to express herself in her own way? Does she know she can do things no one else can do?

Parents also can ask questions that reflect a child's sense of power over his own life. Is the child allowed to make his own decisions? Is he able to carry out plans he has made? Is he able to cope with failures? If any of these answers are no, parents should work with their child to help him develop these important planning and coping skills. Give him the chance to choose between certain options the next time a problem comes up, or encourage him to complete the next project he starts.

Role models can be very influential on children as they carve out their identities. Parents should consider whether the child has the opportunity to interact with people who are worthy models. Does he have the confidence to distinguish right from wrong with the help of these models? Does he have models who help him learn how to accomplish goals? Appropriate role models are critical for children in developing a strong sense of worth. The parent may need to seek role models out if he thinks additional ones are needed.

Parents can effectively raise their child's self-esteem by praising a child in a truthful, descriptive way. For example, first a parent can describe what she sees. "I see a clean floor, a smooth bed, and your books neatly lined on the shelf." Then, the parent can describe what she feels as she praises the child. "It's a pleasure to walk into this room." And lastly, sum up the child's praise-worthy behavior with a word. "You sorted out your pencils, crayons, and pens in separate boxes. That's what I call organization!"

Parents who act as good role models and praise their child when appropriate can enjoy watching their child mature into an individual with a sense of self-worth and confidence in his/her pursuits.

PARENTING POINTERS

➤ In assessing a child's self-esteem, parents should look at a child's relationships with others and confidence in being their own person.

➤ Parents should let children make some decisions for themselves to develop a sense of control over their life.

➤ Exposing children to positive role models can help them discover their own identity and self-worth.

➤ Praising kids in honest and specific ways can enhance their self-esteem.

4. Listening
Tools to help children open up

Everyone likes to be heard — and children are no exception. Listening is an important parenting skill that can help nurture a healthy parent-child relationship and improve one that is not so healthy. When parents take the time to listen, children feel special and loved.

Children need to know that what they feel is important and valued. At times, however, children may have trouble identifying their feelings without some parental nudging. To get kids to open up, parents can start by helping children to think about and to express their feelings. Try something such as, "You seem sad today. Do you want to tell me about it?" This can be done in a non-judgmental way, so children will speak freely without fear of criticism. Parents should listen carefully to help children identify, clarify, and expand on their feelings.

The parent also can act as a mirror, reflecting or restating the feelings back to the child. For example, say, "From what you said, you really are having a hard time getting your friend to take turns. That makes you frustrated." In this way, parents can give children the opportunity to vent their emotions verbally. This way their feelings don't build up to the point where they must be acted out in harmful or disruptive behavior. When parents take children's statements seriously by listening carefully it is a boost to their children's self-esteem, too.

Sometimes it is difficult to focus and truly listen to children. But there are some ways to help parents become more effective listeners.

First, parents should consider the words, body language, tone of voice, and context of what the child says. Then, identify the child's feeling. For example, if the child says, "Nobody ever plays with me," the parent might recognize that he feels lonely, bored, or rejected.

Once the child has expressed his feeling, the parent should accept the feeling as real, and avoid the temptation to try to change it. The parent can verbalize that feeling back to the child in a complete sentence, such as "You're feeling pretty lonely right now." It's best not to ask why he's feeling that way; he'll probably say he doesn't know. Instead, the parent can then attach a reason for his feeling. For example, "You feel lonely because it seems like nobody wants to be your friend." The purpose here is not to give advice but to simply affirm his feeling. The parent can also express empathy and encouragement, saying "I've felt like that before. It's okay, you'll find a friend."

By taking the time to stop and really listen, parents also teach children that they have a right to have and express their own feelings and values. Even if a parent disagrees with his child's behavior, he needs to respect that everyone has a right to his or her own feelings. Also, by reflecting back children's feelings, parents will be showing them a good communication skill that they can use in future relationships with others.

Parents may feel awkward at first when learning to listen and reflect their child's feelings, much the same as they would feel in learning any new skill. With practice it will become more natural and be a definite benefit to everyone. In time the child, too, will get better at clarifying feelings and analyzing his or her personal concerns.

PARENTING POINTERS

➤ Some children need parents to help them identify and express their feelings. Parents can start by acting as a "mirror" to reflect back how they think the child might be feeling.

➤ Listening carefully to children can make them feel important and enhance their self-esteem.

➤ When listening to children, pay attention to their exact words, tone, body language, and the context of what they are saying.

5. Communication
Winning ways to talk with your child

A child can get overly excited to tell a parent all the details of a science project or a soccer game. In the busyness of life, however, a parent doesn't always tune in completely. The parent may catch bits and pieces of the story, half listening while cooking dinner. Unfortunately, when a parent doesn't give a child her full attention, the child can feel rejected. After a while the child may stop sharing her feelings altogether, leaving the parent wondering what went wrong.

Two-way communication is a critical parenting skill that can be mastered with a little effort. It is important for parents to understand that children have special communication needs at different ages. A three-year-old with a thriving imagination can make things up to get a parent's attention or tell stories over and over. It can be boring or annoying, at times, but parents need to be patient. Adolescents, on the other hand, may need to blow off steam. This can spark an argument if parents take the comment personally or jump in and try to fix the situation.

Here are a few practical strategies for parents who want to keep the lines of communication open. First and foremost, parents should make themselves available when their child needs to talk. This is especially important with teens, who may want to talk only rarely. If a parent can't give his full attention on the spot, schedule a time to discuss the situation later.

Get comfortable when talking with a child. Try to sit down and get at the same eye level as the child. This is especially true with toddlers, to whom adults seem like giants.

Next, parents need to be accepting rather than judgmental when communicating with kids; otherwise, the child may not respond. Parents can do this by using statements that show the parent understands the way the child is feeling. For example, a parent can say to a child, "You seem to be feeling frustrated" or "You must be very proud." This approach can help the conversation flow smoothly. In fact, a child may actually solve his own problem by talking it out.

If a child does something that concerns a parent, rather than place blame, a parent can turn things around with an "I" message. For example, a parent can say, "I feel upset when you leave your wet towels on the bed" or "I feel frantic when you don't call and let me know you're going to be late." For sensitive teenagers, it may be effective to communicate in the form of a note or a funny sign too.

Listening and talking with kids takes time, but it will do much to nurture a healthy parent-child relationship. Parents can then follow through after their communication efforts by expressing pleasure for how it went. A parent can say, "I'm so glad we had that discussion. You did a great job letting me know your point of view." This will leave children feeling loved and accepted, equipping them for growth and change throughout life.

PARENTING POINTERS

➤ When talking with children parents should try to give their complete attention.

➤ Try to talk with children at eye level.

➤ Listen and accept children's feelings, this can aid the flow of any conversation.

➤ Take the time to communicate well and to follow up with praise to create a better parent-child relationship.

6. Nurturing
The art of balancing support with discipline

Nurturing can mean to nourish and feed — or to train and educate. It is especially difficult for parents of young children to decide when to be the nurturer/supporter and when to be the trainer/disciplinarian.

Today's smaller nuclear family creates closer and more intense relationships than in the larger family of several generations ago, when grandparents and extended family often lived together and served as substitute parents and role models. Single-parent families are more common now. A more democratic family atmosphere, which is typical of today's families, also can create difficulties in establishing discipline in the home, as parents decide when to stand firm and when to acquiesce to a demanding child.

It can be a challenge to remain consistent. There are many moments of overload, when everyone is hungry, the baby is crying, and the phone is ringing. Also, parents may find they lack certain necessary skills as their children grow and change. Just when parents have the routine down of caring for an infant, they are confronted with the challenge of learning to cope with a raging toddler whose favorite word seems to be "no."

Parents are quick to respond to all the wishes of an infant. But as children become toddlers, parents need to begin to establish appropriate expectations and responsibilities. For example, it may be faster for a parent to dress their toddler, but the child will never learn to put on a shirt by himself if he is not asked to try it. Challenging a child to be more independent can be difficult for parents who want to be liked by their children, since their toddlers inevitably will feel frustrated trying new things and learning what they can and cannot do.

A two-year-old can understand a comment, such as, "It's very hard to wait for dinner when you are hungry, isn't it?" By the time the child is three, it is appropriate to say "When you put your blocks on the shelf, we can go for a walk." Parents should expect the child to do as much as he can for himself while empathizing with him and giving emotional support.

Parents need to help toddlers learn to explain their needs and feelings with words rather than to express frustration by throwing tantrums. This is how children begin to learn the power of language. Saying, "Tell me in words what you want," followed by praise when the request is made, can set the pattern.

It is helpful to be patient and set mutual goals at this stage. Comments such as "Won't it be great when you can finish your meal without spilling your milk?" or "How lucky you'll be when you can keep your pants dry!" are good examples. As for eating battles, how much a child eats is best left to him with as little attention from parents as possible. Eventually he'll eat what he needs, if sweets and between-meal, non-nutritious foods are withheld.

If parents always comply with a child's demands, they will find that she won't be able to face the reality that she's not the all-powerful, magically controlling little person she imagines. On the other hand, if parents ask too much of the child, she'll be afraid to show frustration and anger and may displace her true feelings to an imaginary friend or push them inside. Either way, the child loses. Young children need emotional support to be able to establish self-control and to express both anger and love. All children need parental help to affirm themselves as separate persons with feelings of their own.

From ages three to six children love to make things and pretend. They become an active rather than passive participant, often playing the same scene over and over again. In joint play with parents they love to tell the parent what he should do and who he should be. This is the perfect opportunity for parents to nurture creativity by playing out these roles.

Kids at this age may idolize the parent of the opposite sex while using the same-sex parent as a role model. They can have highly vivid imaginations, so telling the truth is not always easy. They just haven't had enough life experience yet to distinguish truth and reality from fantasy. Nurturing parents can help by offering truthful explanations.

Children in this age group can also offer ideas about how to fulfill parents' expectations. For example, if a parent says, "I'm unhappy about this; what do you think you I can do about it?", children can offer their ideas.

Enrolling a preschooler in a nursery school or play group can also help the child develop by giving her another place to form relationships outside the home. When a new baby arrives in the family, another learning situation develops. Toddlers then discover how to cope with angry feelings and share parental attention. Sensitive to the need to nurture their child, parents can use special times together and "time-outs" to diffuse the situation. For example, a set time each day to read together while the baby naps gives the toddler a chance to express her feelings and the parent a chance to respond with love.

Parents should consider time-outs for themselves as well — time away from their young children that helps them stay balanced. It helps them hone their perspective as parents while remaining attuned to their children's feelings.

PARENTING POINTERS

➤ Parents need to set appropriate expectations for their toddlers, rather than trying to do everything for them.

➤ Children should learn to use words rather than tantrums to express their feelings.

➤ Parents need to be consistent and not always cave in to children's demands.

➤ Parents should provide opportunities for children to develop relationships with friends and others outside the home.

➤ Time-outs can be useful for adults, too.

7. Discipline
Managing a peaceful home

Parents discipline children with the hope that they will grow up to be responsible adults. There are a variety of approaches to discipline that work for families. With some thought — and trial and error — parents can arrive at the right balance of discipline using lessons of consequences and positive rewards.

There are drawbacks to the traditional method of discipline — punishment. In fact, studies show that extreme forms of punishment such as paddling can lead to psychological problems for both the child and parent(s). Punishment expresses the power of personal authority and can leave both the parent and child feeling resentful. In addition, the child learns what to avoid, but not what to do. Punishment can then become a distraction, as the child thinks of revenge strategies rather than learning from the experience.

This is not to say that all punishment is negative or ineffective. Sometimes parents can create artificial consequences for bad behavior. One such consequence would be depriving a child of something that's important to her, like a TV program or staying up late. Another consequence might be social isolation, such as sending a child away from the group to her room.

Applying natural and logical consequences to a child's behavior at any age can be a very effective approach to discipline. This approach holds the child, not the parents, responsible for the child's behavior. As in the real world, the child suffers the consequences of his own behavior. For example, if an adult is late for work consistently, she may get poor job reviews. If a child is consistently late for his ride to school, he may have to walk and arrive late, receiving a tardy slip. A younger child may lose her treat if she insists on throwing it over the fence. The goal is to use logical consequences to motivate a child to make responsible decisions, rather than forcing the child to obey a parent.

Natural consequences often are related to the misbehavior. For example, if a child refuses to use good table manners, he may be excluded from the family dinner table to eat by himself in the kitchen. When applying logical consequences, parents need to give a verbal choice to their child and then accept his decision and follow through with the consequence. "Since you've decided to continue playing with your food, you'll need to sit in the kitchen." The child must know why and for what behavior they are being punished. It must not appear arbitrary.

Another way to influence kids' behavior is the positive reward system. Children of any age prefer positive attention. By following wanted behavior with a positive reward a parent can encourage the child to repeat it. For example, if a child displays good table manners, praise and a hug can be offered. As the behavior is learned and repeated, the rewards can be spaced out. Rewards need to be within reasonable limits, of course, so that children don't learn to beg. While using this positive reward system, a parent might ignore negative behavior unless it's harmful or destructive.

When parents start focusing on the positive aspects of their child, they often catch her doing something right. But, it's unrealistic to expect proper behavior all the time if it's not reinforced. After all, would an adult want to fix a nice meal if no one acknowledged it? A child feels the same way. She likes her good efforts to be acknowledged.

Establishing rules is another key to good management at home. Rules help a child feel secure and to know the limits and consequences of their behavior. Rules also teach responsibility. To be effective, rules must be reasonable and consistent. In addition, too many or too few rules may create confusion. Rules should be described in detail, with consequences outlined and enforced.

Another method of discipline is to arrange contract agreements between parents and children. In such contracts, a child promises to do a particular thing, and parents promise to do something in return. For example, a child who is having difficulty completing practice sessions on a musical instrument can negotiate with his parent the time he needs to practice each day before he watches his favorite TV show. Perhaps if he practices thirty minutes each school day, he will be able to watch thirty minutes of TV. Everyone wins and the child is rewarded for his good behavior.

These discipline and management techniques develop responsible, self-disciplined children. They are based on mutual respect between parent and child and promote healthy interchanges and problem solving.

PARENTING POINTERS

➤ Using only punishment to discipline children focuses children on avoiding certain behaviors and can lead to resentment.

➤ Children learn lessons of responsibility in the real world when parents allow children to suffer the consequences of their own behavior.

➤ When parents give children positive rewards for good behavior, children are encouraged to repeat the good works.

➤ Children need to understand rules, expectations, and the consequences for not complying.

➤ Negotiating agreements between parents and children can be an effective method of discipline.

8. Birth order

How it affects temperament and behavior

Children from the same family often display unique differences in temperament and behavior. This can be explained by genetics and changing environments, as well as birth order within the family. To better understand each of their children, it helps for parents to learn the strengths and limitations associated with being the oldest, youngest, or middle child. (While descriptions of children by birth order are useful, these generalizations don't always apply. Becoming aware, however, of these traits and behaviors common to birth order can be helpful. As always, parents should tune in and respond to the unique characteristics of each child as an individual.)

In general, first-born children tend to be high achievers. Since first-time parents can be anxious, apprehensive and demanding, their children are affected. First-born children get the full love and attention of their parents, but they are also subject to strong expectations of family standards and values. They feel the full brunt of parental pressure to succeed.

First-born children usually are successful in school and can be described as competent and almost always compliant. They can also be bossy and rigid. Generally, first-borns learn faster than other siblings and approach life more seriously. Historically, because they spend so much time with other adults, they talk in a more adult way.

When the next sibling arrives, all children experience some jealousy until they realize that the parents are still there for them. The second child may also be the youngest child in the family with the characteristics of that position. But, some are true "middle children" with their special attributes.

With parents less available to them than to first-borns, middle children seem to be more laid back and relaxed. Sometimes they need to be a bit manipulative to satisfy their needs. They are also good diplomats and quite friendly. They often use their position in the middle to be peacemakers.

The intensity of their struggle for identity as a middle child will depend on the sex of the child. If they are the same sex as the first-born, the struggle will be more pronounced. Middle children sometimes feel they need to work hard to achieve uniqueness and get ahead. They are very concerned with fairness and may have difficulty with social interactions with peers. Since many first-borns excel in academics, second-borns often excel in sports.

The youngest child in the family frequently has special privileges and gains considerable social skills because of her interactions with older siblings. She is often charming, lighthearted, and playful. She does have a need to be nurtured and sometimes has difficulty in accepting responsibility.

Only children comprise their own category. Their dependence on parents often keeps them closer to parents into adulthood. With total parental attention, they are uniquely self-confident, usually do well in school, and often feel special. Only children tend to have a sense of responsibility to the world and do not need a sense of competition to do their best. Only children often become leaders and achieve high positions in the world.

Birth order, like every other factor in the development of the child, differs from the norm for individual children. A child of any birth position may or may not exhibit these characteristics, but understanding the common differences can be useful as parents try to understand each child's uniqueness.

PARENTING POINTERS

➤ First-born children, who often receive the most parental pressure to succeed, tend to comply with authority and are high achievers.

➤ Middle-children need to establish separate identities from their older siblings. They often are not as intense but, rather, are good at compromising and in forming relationships with others.

➤ In general, the youngest children develop good people skills, but they also have more difficulty accepting responsibility.

➤ While common traits based on birth order do exist, parents should be careful to treat each child as an individual.

9. Realistic expectations
How to gear expectations toward a child's stage of development

It's almost impossible to avoid comparing a child's development with that of his peers. When a parent picks up her child at day care and sees another toddler naming colors, she may think, "Why isn't mine?" If the five-year-old child next door listens much better, a parent may think, "Why is my child so spoiled?"

Parents are programmed to look for childhood milestones at specific ages. Gearing parental expectations to a child's chronological age is a trap that catches many parents. A much better way to assess progress is to consider the child's developmental age. Chronological age is simply the number of years and months from the child's birth date. Developmental age is a broader concept that encompasses physical, emotional, intellectual, perceptual, language, and other skills.

Not all children of the same chronological age develop at the same rate. Most kids begin to read at age six, for example, but the normal range for reading readiness is between ages four and eight. And, development doesn't always occur evenly. A five-year-old with exceptional verbal skills may still function emotionally at a five-year-old or younger level. An eight-year-old may have the intellectual development of a ten-year-old and the agility of a seven-year-old.

Comparing children to their peers or with advice of books and well-meaning neighbors can set a child up for failure or encourage low self-esteem. No matter how much they want to please, children can't master certain skills and behaviors until they're developmentally ready. Children can sense parental concerns and pressures and become worried and self-conscious about their inability to please them. They may try harder, while their own anxiety gets in the way and they fail. This can create an unfortunate and hard-to-break pattern of failure.

For example, a father may ask his son to play baseball and then criticize him for not performing well. However, the child may not yet have developed the hand-eye coordination necessary to pitch or bat a ball. The parent's criticism can lead to a poor self-image and possibly to other more serious problems in the parent-child relationship.

Parents need to understand that kids develop at their own pace, not always according to a specific age. Just by talking to other parents, a parent can learn that not all children develop along a straight, predictable line. Teachers, pediatricians, and child development texts can help inform parents about the broad time periods during which children develop and master skills.

Parents can gear their expectations about home behaviors — for doing chores, obeying, sharing — to their child's developmental age as well. This helps reduce the friction that occurs if parents expect too much compliance from a very young child.

The bottom line is to recognize when a behavior changes and then incorporate that into the context of where a child is in terms of his development. Then, a parent can set realistic expectations based on the child's capabilities. If a child seems to lag, a parent should focus on his or her strengths, not deficits. The end result will be confident children and a happier home.

PARENTING POINTERS

➤ Parents should remember that not all children progress at the same rate. A child's developmental age is a better measure than chronological age.

➤ Focus on a child's achievements, rather than areas in which she may be lagging.

➤ Parents can design tasks at home for a child to complete that are appropriate for her developmental level.

➤ By talking with teachers, doctors and other parents, families can discover ranges, rather than specific ages, that children advance.

10. A peaceful home
Ten tips for effective parenting

Most parents want a home where things run smoothly, at least most of the time. Achieving this is not really so complicated. These guidelines can help parents create a peaceful home. Underlying all these tips, the most important advice is to love your child.

1. Clearly define rules and consequences. Children like the structure created by appropriate rules. They feel best when parents are clear about expectations. Keep rules brief and be sure that children can actually follow them. If possible, let children help establish the rules and determine the consequences. Parents may be surprised at what kids come up with . . . often very fair and appropriate consequences.

2. Be consistent enforcing rules. Even though it takes time, parents need to explain to children why rules exist and emphasize the importance of following them. Inconsistency about enforcement of rules only makes children uncertain about the rule's existence and importance. For example, tell a teenager that the reason she has a curfew of 11 p.m. is because you are concerned about her safety on the streets late at night. However, if she is allowed to come in at 11:30 or midnight without any punishment, she will assume the rule isn't to be taken seriously.

3. Establish a predictable routine for children. Children are more cooperative when they understand what to expect during the day. Confusion tires both parents and children. It only takes a few moments to review the day's schedule with children at bedtime or in the morning. Younger kids may need to be reminded of what's going to happen closer to the time of their first activity.

4. Ignoring certain behaviors can be most effective. Surprisingly, negative behaviors that are minor by nature often go away if parents work at ignoring them. Sometimes, however, it takes more time, so don't give up easily. Consistency always pays off. Very negative behaviors, such as truancy, drug use, or breaking the law, on the other hand, need more immediate responses.

5. Tell children clearly what behavior is expected. Children need behaviors and expectations explained to them in clear and simple language. They also do well when parents themselves model that behavior. Children are much more likely to do as parents do than to do as parents say. For instance, if swearing is off limits for children, parents need to abide by the same standards.

6. Catch them being good. Find many opportunities for praise and positive attention. Most parents are quick to point out faults and poor behavior, but it's just as important to point out the good things children do. When children know that their "good" behavior is appreciated, they're much more likely to repeat it. Try to find several good areas to appreciate in your kids each day. For example, when you see two siblings playing a game well together say how nice it is to see them getting along. This can be more effective than jumping in only to break up a disagreement.

7. Avoid lectures and threats. When behavior is inappropriate, say little, but act. When children are involved in disapproved behavior, such as screaming for a cookie, move them physically to another place; divert their attention in some way, or give them some "time out" to regain control.

8. Separate the child's feelings from his behavior. Children can't control the feelings they have, but they can learn to control how they act because of them. For example, it's okay to feel angry with the new baby, but it's not okay to hit your sibling. Explain to kids that it's okay to feel a certain way but not to act in a way that hurts another.

9. Let children learn through natural consequences when possible. If a child loses the parts of a game, he will discover that he can't play with it. Or, if an older child comes in from play late for a meal, have the child eat the food as is or fix something simple for himself; he'll soon learn that parents prepare the family meal only once.

10. Avoid possible problems by anticipating stressful situations for children. Parents know better than anyone else what situations will cause problems for their children. Anticipate the problem before it occurs and brainstorm about ways to diffuse negative reactions. For example, knowing that a child has difficulty getting along with a certain cousin, a parent can discuss what might occur in advance of a visit and offer suggestions for cooperative play.

11. Professional guidance
Determining when families should seek outside help

Most parents face challenging periods with their children. But sometimes parents wonder if they should seek professional help for their child's behavior problems or emotional difficulties. Here are some guidelines to consider when thinking about whether family counseling would be beneficial.

First, a parent's feeling of being "uncomfortable" with the situation is an important indicator that outside help may be warranted. Parents need to trust their instincts. Children don't come with a handbook, but they do come with instinctual messages for parents. Parents may worry that they are overreacting, but if a situation causes a parent discomfort, it deserves attention. Before panicking, perhaps a parent can check with another parent or family member to confirm their feelings and for another opinion. But don't rely solely on the opinion of others. Gut feelings are often correct. If the uncomfortable feelings persist, the parent can seek professional guidance.

Second, a change in the child's behavior, appearance, or values can indicate a need for help. Some examples are changes in eating or sleeping habits, not getting along with friends, frequent crying or unhappiness, or, for a school age child, not being able to achieve in ways consistent with his developmental stage and ability. Of course, change is relative, so parents need to consider how long the behavior has been present. For example, a parent of a child who's been cranky since birth may not be concerned about a particular period of crankiness, but a parent of a child having difficulty sleeping for the first time may be concerned.

Any change in the family system, such as a move, change of job, death, or ongoing conflict among significant adults can cause behavior changes that may merit counseling. For example, if one parent is ill or in the hospital, a family may benefit from learning specific strategies about how to talk about the situation.

If a parent feels uncomfortable about a change in the child's behavior, the parent should look at his own actions before seeking help. It could be that the parent's actions have already begun to make a difference. Upon review, the parent may realize that he's on the right track and just needs to give his strategies more time to work. For example, a parent may be concerned that a child is not completing his schoolwork. When the parent examines the situation, he may find that his daily encouragement is paying off and the child is keeping up.

It's normal to have concerns about parenting. Questioning whether a certain approach is working doesn't necessarily mean that there is a serious problem. Perhaps a parent just needs other sources to reassure him that he's doing the right thing. Seeking family counseling can provide such a sounding board, with information and strategies for parenting.

Adults often parent the way they were raised. However, times change; needs change; and strategies change. Just because you are not parenting the way your parents did, doesn't mean that you are parenting poorly. Parents may simply need affirmation of their parenting competence by a caring family counselor. In addition, a family counseling session may offer parents seeking help a chance to find a parenting style that fits. Parents can then feel confident in their own choice of strategies.

PARENTING POINTERS

➤ Parents should trust their instincts. Feeling uncomfortable with a situation can be an indication that professional guidance is merited.

➤ Significant changes in a child's behavior can signal a need for outside help.

➤ When parents review their own efforts to address the situation, they may discover that they are making progress and professional help is not necessary.

12. It takes a village ...
Parenting all children

Today parents are struggling to raise children amid all sorts of social, economic, and domestic pressures. Many parents lack the support of an extended family. If parents are to raise healthy, happy children, they need help from other parents, neighbors, professionals, even caring strangers.

Most would agree that "It takes a village to raise a child." Parenting all children — whether they need a hug, a bandage, or a reprimand — isn't a new idea. In simpler times people lived close to their relatives and community bonds were tight. Grandma patched up a scraped knee if mom was busy, and an uncle didn't hesitate to deliver an impromptu manners lesson if dad wasn't around. Friends and neighbors weren't shy about pitching in either; there were eyes and ears everywhere. A kid who acted up at the corner drugstore would likely be in trouble the next day because someone had called mom and dad.

For today's mobile and often stressed families, the absence of extended family is a real deprivation. This makes the neighborhood more important for children than ever. Neighbors can provide an additional place where a kid can go to share her hurts as well as her joys. Neighbors can also serve as role models and give kids an alternative frame of reference. Something as simple as having dinner at a neighbor's house can be important for a child. It may help a child discover another family's traditions and perspectives, too.

Children can also feel a sense of community through involvement with a church, school group, or sports team. Parents can help their children choose groups that they feel will have a positive influence on their children. Sometimes the bonds formed with these groups can be as close as family. Coaches, teachers, and church members can serve as role models and mentors.

Adults have a tremendous responsibility to set examples for children. If adults do the right thing, children will only know the right thing. If children watch adults cheat, denigrate others, or keep things that don't belong to them, children will think it's okay to do the same.

In addition to serving as good examples, adults need to let children know when behavior is unacceptable. For example, when a parent is watching a neighbor's child, he becomes essentially the surrogate parent. That neighbor's family depends on the parent to keep the child safe, and to discipline the child with authority but without damaging his dignity. When a visiting child misbehaves, a parent might say firmly, "That isn't okay in our house. That's against our house rules."

Adults can make a difference in the lives of children, when they consider their personal responsibility to be good examples and to intervene for kid's sake.

PARENTING POINTERS

➤ In today's mobile society when many families live away from relatives, parents can reach out to neighbors and others in the community to serve as a support system.

➤ Children can gain from the mentoring of other responsible adults, such as neighbors, church leaders, or coaches.

➤ Adults have an obligation to be good role models for children and intervene when appropriate.

➤ Children who are raised by a community learn to have respect for the community.

11

Nurturing the Young Child

13. Play
Having fun is an important part of learning

Play is the work of children, a time in which they build the skills necessary to grow and gain self-confidence. When children play, it is their way of learning and developing. Playing with kids and watching them develop is one of the true joys of parenting.

A baby struggles to crawl, walk, and climb. For a one-year-old, playing the same game over and over, such as peek-a-boo, is a way of mastering sensory and physical skills.

Children age two to five often play by imitating their parents or older children. They play dress-up or pretend to cook. In trying on the role of another, children are working hard to see the world from another person's perspective.

After age three, imaginary play dominates. A child can create short scenes or whole fantasy stories in a cardboard carton or sandbox. He takes an active role in the play and controls the events that he creates. Often he is playing out experiences that have some anxiety for him. Hide-and-seek, for example, may be a way of replaying the anxiety of having a loved one leave and then reappear, but this time the child is making it happen.

Pretending to be a hero — a princess, superman, or astronaut — helps the child to extend her boundaries and to see herself as more than a dependent child. It also offers the chance to release pent-up energy and emotion in a safe, productive manner. As children carry out fantasy play scenes they develop verbal skills and humor. This sort of play is a step toward learning the power of the word over the power of the fist.

Kids seem to be naturally drawn to animals. Pretending to be an animal, such as roaring tiger or a galloping horse, is a great way for a child to be creative. It can also be a safe, productive way for children to express themselves and deal with relationships.

Imaginary play with other children also helps children make friends and build social skills. Following and giving directions, learning to take turns, and helping another child are important lessons. Each child must learn to accept being a leader of a group, following a group, as well as being excluded from a social clique.

When parents and children play together it can be rewarding for both. The parent can serve as a role model for the child. However, if the parent takes over the play, it's no longer fun for the child. A child needs warning that soon it will be time to end the play and return to the usual roles.

From ages three to adulthood, board and card games help children deal with numbers, matching, and colors. Learning how to plan ahead and to execute strategy is an important part of checkers, chess or Monopoly. Games also teach children lessons about handling winning and losing. Young children, who can't seem to tolerate losing and upset the Candyland board when they think they might not win, will soon find that the fun of playing together is more important than always winning. They will learn that the fun of friendship is better than always being "number one."

Children often pick someone to play with who mirrors some quality that the child would like in themselves. For instance, a shy child may pick a bossy friend. Parents may not like it, but they need to respect the child's choice and, as a result of the friendship, the child may become more assertive. Play is as critical to children as any work adults perform, and besides, it's fun.

PARENTING POINTERS
➤ Children learn and develop through play.
➤ Through imitation and imagination kids can understand other people's perspectives and deal with their own anxieties.

➤ Parents should play with their children, but not dominate the activity.

➤ Kids need a warning before play ends.

➤ Games can teach kids the fun of winning and how to handling losing with grace.

14. Fears

Helping kids cope through understanding and imagination

Everyone has fears and concerns. After all, fear is a safety mechanism and a certain amount of fear is healthy. However, children need help in learning to deal with fears, especially when the fears extend over a long period or interfere with activities. Parents and caregivers can help children conquer worries by tuning into children's concerns and offering support.

Children fear various things at different ages. Infants and toddlers may be afraid of loud noises or strangers, while preschoolers may fear dark places, make-believe creatures, or sleeping alone. School-age children may begin to be concerned with death and war. Adolescents may fear rejection from peers. Even adults have fears. A recent study from Harvard University confirms that ten percent of the population is predisposed to fearfulness. Children who are innately fearful approach the world cautiously. Timid and shy by nature, many children need extra support with conquering fears.

Fear can be triggered by something a child sees, such as lightning hitting a tree. Understanding why things happen can help kids confront and overcome scary situations. With the help of a sympathetic parent, children learn to overcome fear and gain new confidence — important for emotional growth.

As a parent, it is important to first recognize what the child is experiencing and try to start a dialogue. Wait for a clue from the child that he is ready to try to address his fear. Parents should never force the issue. Then pick the best time to sit down and talk with the child.

Instead of asking a question, try to define the child's feelings. Start by asking, "You seem so sad, you're afraid of lightning." Don't ask, "Why are you afraid?" Reflecting what the child is feeling is often enough for the child to begin to open up and explain his feelings.

Whatever the source, children need to be able to express fears. Often talking unburdens the child, as she leaves her concern with the adult. Parents need to listen, not judge. Telling children not to be afraid robs them of the opportunity to learn from the experience. Yelling or punishing doesn't help either. As children talk about experiences and feelings, they can often come up with their own solutions about how to overcome their fears.

Parents, too, can serve as models of how to confront a scary situation, as long as they don't share the same fear. If they do, another adult or other children can help. Slowly, in small steps, the fear can be conquered. Sometimes these steps are playing imaginary games, reading books, or making up situations to help children get closer to the actual fear. Remember to give verbal praise and rewards for each step.

Imagination is the most important way young children can address fears. It helps them understand themselves, gain control over their world, and build self-esteem. Play and imagination make fears "touchable." Children can create new situations the way they would like things to be. For example, a child can replay a fight between parents or siblings and give it a peaceful resolution. Or, if they're anxious or fearful about a situation, they may just need to experience it through play to overcome the stress.

With imagination, children can become what they fear in order to manage it. They can pretend to be witches, monsters, doctors, moms, dads, neighbors, or teachers. Then they can experience their fears while gaining a sense of control over their world.

Kids need time to use their imaginations. A little girl placing her stuffed animals on a swing set in her make-believe world is being creative and making her own decisions. This makes her feel special and unique as an individual. If they're too booked with activities they won't have time to explore and conquer fears.

The end result is that when fear is addressed both parent and child have grown together. With patience, understanding, and imagination parents can help children conquer fears and move forward.

➤ Acknowledge children's fear. Listen, don't judge.

➤ Encourage children to talk about their feelings, but don't push the subject.

➤ Model, as a parent, ways to address scary situations.

➤ Use imagination and role playing to act out fears.

15. Separation anxiety
Strategies for easing the transition

Toddlers struggle with needing their parents and wanting to explore the world independently. One moment they may be clinging to their parents, the next moment they are off on their own. When a child can understand his identity apart from the parent and be separated without feeling anxious, it is a milestone for both parent and child.

A preschooler needs to test her new self-awareness and ability to do tasks independently. Physically, she has started to do tasks such as dressing and feeding herself. Still, she's not completely comfortable with this sense of being on her own. She's starting to understand she's separate from everyone else in the world, too, but still wants a parent there for comfort.

Preschoolers adjust best to new situations — nursery school or staying with a baby-sitter — in small doses, working up to longer periods. Parents need to talk through the situation with their children. Kids may be worried about what a parent is doing when they are separated, and whether mom and dad will come back. It's a good idea for parents to explain exactly where they'll be and what they'll be doing and assure the child they will return soon.

If it's appropriate for the situation, sometimes a phone call to touch base can be reassuring to the parent. At this point, the caregiver can reassure the child that their parents are coming soon. Talk this over with the caregiver. In some situations, it could be disruptive. Parents need to exercise good judgment. Just as the infant's game of peek-a-boo taught him that people who disappear do come back, experiences of short separation will teach him that parents will come back.

Parents should try to keep the actual good-bye short and sweet. Talk over a good routine with the caregiver. First, be sure the child is settled in her new environment. Offer a hug and a kiss. Then tell the child to have a good day and remind her that you'll be back to get her after her afternoon nap, for instance. Try not to linger, even if the child is crying. Children adapt quickly and will likely stop crying soon after the parent leaves.

A child's special object, such as a stuffed animal or blanket, can be comforting at bedtime and can help the child's transition from home to day care or home to play groups. It can help a preschooler cope with stress to have special objects and imaginary friends to accompany him. If the situation permits, add a note in a lunch or have a child bring a family photo. Objects that have familiar smells and touch do a lot to allay a newly independent toddler's fear of venturing into the unknown. He may need the comfort of the object to remind him of his infancy and security it entailed, just as much as he needs the chance to gain independence and do things his way.

With patience and understanding of the young child's ambivalent feelings about being separated, parents can help him make a successful transition to being a separate, independent, and happy individual.

PARENTING POINTERS

➤ If possible, ease into new situations, such as day care, in small doses.

➤ Parents should explain to children what will happen while they are apart and reassure them they will return soon.

➤ Transitional objects, such as stuffed animals, can comfort a child while he is separated from a parent.

16. Temper tantrums
Understanding and taming the rage

Any parent who has experienced the rage of a toddler's temper tantrum knows the frustration for everyone involved. The child is upset, red-faced, screaming, and out of control. The parent, who is often taken off guard, is forced to take swift action.

Anger is a powerful emotion in both children and adults. Yet most adults have the advantage of greater discipline and self-control when handling their anger. Children can be overwhelmed by their angry feelings. What starts out as a minor objection to an adult's simple command can turn into a major explosion because the child lacks the ability to cope with conflict successfully.

Tantrums usually occur between the ages of two and four. Two-year-olds begin to feel a strong surge of independence. Walking has been mastered, communication is emerging, and a strong sense of identity is developing. The child also may discover that he has some degree of control over his parents, so he exercises it. He wants to do things himself and in his own way — **now**. Since parents must often overrule children in the interests of safety and common sense, conflict is inevitable.

It's important to remember that children's anger is natural and normal, and they have a right to feel it and express it. Parents must find a way to let children express their anger without becoming violent or destructive. Pre-verbal children, who have a tendency to hit, may be given a substitute object such as a pillow to hit. Older children may find talking is a good way to release anger. Simply stating that they are mad and why will help diffuse the anger. Quite often, in the course of such a conversation, the anger begins to diminish and misunderstandings that caused the incident are cleared up.

Often, a child out of control in a tantrum is very frightened to find out she can't control her own aggression and may be relieved to have parents intervene. Children also feel safer when they know that they're not allowed to be destructive. Distracting a child from controversial activity is a good way to reduce the likelihood of a tantrum. Rather than saying "no" or "don't do that," a parent can take the child by the hand and suggest another activity. Many potential crises can be averted through redirecting.

For older children, reasoning often works. Parents can quietly explain that they don't like the angry behavior and will be happy to talk about solutions after the child calms down. By age four, children begin to negotiate on a more cognitive level, and the incidents of violent outbursts usually decrease.

PARENTING POINTERS

➤ During temper tantrums parents should not touch the child, but remain near by.

➤ It is important not give in to the outraged child. Capitulating will only reinforce that angry displays get him what he wants.

➤ When a temper tantrum occurs remove the child from the situation. For example, if a child screams for his way at a shopping center, take him to the car immediately. Consistency will reinforce this.

➤ Parents should stay calm during tantrums. A parent's behavior sets up a pattern for the child's future behavior. The calmer the parent stays, the faster the incident passes.

17. Sleep disturbances
Bedtime routines to make it through the night

Putting children to sleep is an art that many parents never truly master. We often rock, read, sing, soothe, and even plead and prod our children into dreamland. Once the child drifts off to sleep, the parent can breathe a sigh of relief. But for many, the relief lasts only a short time. All too often children stir in the night, waking up the entire household crying before slipping into mom and dad's bedroom for comfort.

Difficulty sleeping can mean a change in a child's sleep pattern, difficulty in going to sleep, or staying asleep. Sleep problems occur fairly frequently in young children, especially during times of developmental milestones, such as walking, talking, etc. Parents can start to address the situation by looking for the causes. Then parents can try various strategies and routines to ease the transition to sleep.

Parents can expect young infants to have unpredictable sleep patterns. Eventually children begin to regulate their sleep, but sleep problems can be caused by a number of things. Toddlers sometimes begin to have trouble sleeping during the time of toilet training. This can be a signal to parents that he feels pressured. It might be a good idea to be flexible about the timing for toilet training and to try again at a later date. Preschoolers may experience problems in going to sleep or staying asleep when they hear disturbing stories or see TV shows with upsetting images, such as monsters and dragons. These dangers can be very real and frightening to them. Parents need to be reassuring and supportive. Explain again and again that the creatures are imaginary. A small light in the bedroom often helps, but be careful that it doesn't throw off scary shadows.

During the elementary school years, there are many reasons why children may have trouble sleeping. The cause could be medical, emotional, or even the result of parenting. Parents should stop and reflect on how the bedtime routine is carried out in their home. Sometimes parents, through no fault of their own, feel very anxious about the child who won't go to sleep or stay asleep. They can indirectly communicate this tension to the child and make the child feel more stressed, which exacerbates the sleep disturbance.

Parents can ask, "What is our bedtime routine each night — pajamas, story, brushing teeth, prayers, good night kiss? Do we follow this routine consistently? Is bedtime at our house a pleasant time? Are we relaxed or rushed? Do the children seem to enjoy it? Do we enjoy it?"

Consistency at bedtime is important. Children feel more secure when they know what to anticipate. They like to have their routines and rituals in the same order each night. If a parent is fatigued or stressed and tries to eliminate the snack or story, it may disturb the child.

Sweet snacks at bedtime may also contribute to sleep problems. Instead of candy or cookies, try a glass of milk and a few crackers. The protein in the milk can help to prevent a drop in blood sugar, a frequent cause of wakefulness. Also avoid too much activity just before bed, such as rough-housing or tickling games. This applies to action-oriented TV too. Parents should convey to the child that there's a definite time for sleep. This can be done kindly but firmly. In some cases, parents need to insist that the child stay in his or her room at night and not wander downstairs with half a dozen requests.

When a child wakes up during the night, take him back to bed quietly and soothe him. Do not play or read stories. A few comforting words should be all that's necessary. It's not a good idea for the child to get into bed with parents or for the parent to lie down in the child's bed. This can make the middle-of-the-night meeting so warm and comfy that the child will want to repeat it each night.

A sleep disturbance becomes a real problem when the parents begin to feel stressed and it has been going on for a long time. The chronic fatigue generated by a child who doesn't sleep well can cause tension in a marriage, inefficiency at work, academic problems, and general disharmony in the home. If the problem persists over several weeks or months, the parents may want to consult their pediatrician. This would be warranted if the sleep problems result in a change in the child's functioning during the day. With a chronic problem, the pediatrician may want to see if there is a medical reason for the sleeplessness.

Parents should be careful not to overreact to an occasional incident of sleep disturbance. Sleeplessness that occurs once in a while is a typical reaction to excitement, a new school, or a new friend.

Most sleep disturbances can be corrected quickly. Sleep is precious and vital to all members of the family. Once the sleep problem is resolved, the family can move forward — with rested minds and bodies — and continue to grow together.

PARENTING POINTERS

➤ Parents need to assess possible causes of sleeping problems before taking action.

➤ Children do best when established bedtime routines are followed.

➤ Children sleep better when they avoid sweet snacks or active play just before bed.

➤ When children do wake up in the night, parents should briefly comfort them with reassuring words and return them to bed.

18. Toilet training
Timing and patience are keys to success

Most parents can't wait for the day when they don't have to change another diaper. They are eager to start their child on the path to using the toilet. Yet, toddlers don't always share the same enthusiasm. They are at the stage where they need to assert themselves as independent thinkers. A parent's request of "Try this" or "Come over here" is often greeted with a loud and clear "No!" from the child. A struggle of wills can result, making toilet training a challenge. At the right time and with patience, however, a parent can help a child master this skill. The child will gain a sense of accomplishment and self-confidence.

The most important thing is to decide if the child is ready to master this task. She must be physically ready. Before children are 18 months their muscles aren't developed enough to control bowel movements. Starting too early is asking for failure. Between the ages of 18 and 30 months chances for success increase, as children are better able to understand and follow directions.

By the age of two-and-a-half toddlers love to imitate adult behaviors. They may be transfixed by watching peers and siblings use the toilet. Children enjoy being praised for correct bathroom routines. However, remember that every child is different. Look for cues that your child is ready to start. For example, a child who can stay dry all night or for long periods is demonstrating increased bladder control. He may begin to express discomfort when the diaper is wet with comments such as "They're yucky." A child needs good verbal skills to be able to tell a parent when he needs to go. He should also be able to follow one direction at a time. A child also may indicate readiness by showing curiosity in the toilet and trying to sit on it.

Parents should be patient during this process. There is no set time-table for success. It is natural for children to have accidents and regress from time to time while learning this new skill. This doesn't mean that they're defiant or undisciplined. It simply means the task is a difficult one and the child is normal. Parents need to praise children when they are successful, but not punish them when there are setbacks.

If a child seems to be excessively nervous or anxious about the process, don't push it. It may be better to wait for a few weeks before trying again. A child won't respond simply because a parent is pressuring him; he must be willing to try and demonstrate some initiative. Parents should be calm and matter of fact about the natural ups and downs of toilet training, while encouraging and praising the child for his progress.

Helping a child learn to use the toilet is a chance for a parent to allow the child take charge of her own body and to master a task with confidence. And both parent and child should share in the success. The key is to approach the situation at the right time with an abundance of patience. In the end, it is definitely a win-win situation.

PARENTING POINTERS

➤ Physically, children are not ready to start toilet training before the age of 18 months. Between 18 and 30 months the chance for success increases.

➤ Look for signs the child is ready, such as curiosity watching others in the bathroom.

➤ Parents should expect setbacks and respond calmly.

➤ Children need praise for their accomplishments, not punishment, during the toilet training process.

19. The active, strong-willed child
Strategies for parenting high-energy children

Some children are more active and strong-willed than others: it's simply their personality to be on the go and to be sure about what they want to do. Parents who don't have the same energy level may become frustrated or worn out.

Highly spirited kids are simply more of everything. Emotions are deep and powerful. When gleeful, they really shout, and when tearful, they wail. They approach activities with intensity, and their emotional reactions tend to be elevated. They are persistent in their endeavors and find it difficult to switch gears once focused. These kids tend to create their own schedules and may overreact to changes in routine. They need a calm parent to guide them and provide structure.

Parenting these children can be a challenge, but there are strategies that can help. For example, when a strong-willed child is asked to stop an activity, she doesn't easily let go. She may need to be warned that a change will soon take place before the time comes. Talk with the child about ideas that might help her stop, such as blinking the lights when it's time to finish. A parent can fend off a dramatic reaction with a comment such as, "Today's playtime is over, but we can do that again tomorrow." Parents should be calm and recognize that it can be really difficult for the child to stop. Moody responses are actually a reflection of their intense focus on the activity.

The key is to provide an overall structure, not a precise schedule, for children's activities. Parents should explain what is coming next to avoid surprises. When facing a new activity that the child may reject, give her time to observe and remind her of similar situations that turned out to be pleasing.

High-energy children should not be confused with children that are diagnosed as clinically hyperactive. Clinically hyperactive children also may be very active, but their inability to sit still is almost a constant. Clinical hyperactivity is also characterized by distractibility, with the child unable to listen for long or easily complete tasks. (Parents should consult a physician if they suspect a child is extremely hyperactive.)

Most high-energy children are normally active, but still cause their parents some frustration. Parents should provide these children with acceptable outlets for their energy. Physical activities, such as running, jumping and climbing, can be a healthy way to release their intensity. But kids can be over-stimulated, so activities should have limits.

If parents notice that active children are beginning to get too wound up, they can provide activities that soothe and calm, such as rocking, bedtime stories, and quiet games. Remember, too, that children need to be protected from too much stimulation, such as bright lights, noises, or too much TV. Most important, parents need to accept an active, strong-willed child's personality and enjoy the rewards of the child's success and development.

PARENTING POINTERS

➤ Some children are more active and strong-willed by personality type than others.

➤ Parents should first accept the high energy level of these children and help them manage their activity load.

➤ Parents can help strong-willed children adapt by explaining activities and providing somewhat flexible schedules.

➤ Be aware when a child is getting over stimulated and switch to calm activities, such as reading or rocking.

➤ Parents need to provide healthy, physical outlets for children's energy.

➤ A child who is diagnosed as clinically hyperactive also is easily distracted and has trouble completing tasks.

20. A new sibling
Preparing children for baby's arrival

Preparing a toddler for the arrival of a new sibling is a challenge, but there are steps parents can take to ease the transition. It's generally best to share the news early, because young children overhear conversations and pick up "vibes." Rather than have the child feel confused or anxious about what's going to happen, it's best to prepare them early on. Parents may want to wait a couple of months, however, until the risk of miscarriage has passed.

Parents should explain that it will be a long time before the new baby comes — like waiting for Christmas or for a birthday. Just as it takes the mother nine months to adjust to the idea, kids need time too. Talk with the child about things he will do with the new baby, such as going to the park. Answer any questions as honestly as possible. Reassure the older child that she will always be very special and very loved.

As the pregnancy progresses and becomes obvious, a mother may allow the child to pat her tummy and feel the baby's movement. If the children are told that the baby is growing in a warm, safe place inside mother until he or she is ready to be born, the whole process seems more real.

Parents can try to involve their young child in the preparations for the new baby. The child can make choices about what color the baby's blanket will be or what special new toy will be put in the baby's room. Once the baby arrives, the child can hold the newborn and help give the baby a bottle — with the help of an adult.

Visiting mom after the delivery can be a very positive experience as well. Preschoolers often have misconceptions about hospitals. Seeing mom and seeing the new baby reassures them that everybody is okay. Perhaps the older child could have a small gift for the new baby when he visits the hospital.

The homecoming can be particularly tough on a toddler who will now feel displaced because of the baby. The older sibling may wonder if his parents got a new baby because they weren't satisfied with him. It's very natural for the older children in the family to be jealous of the new brother or sister. This type of hurt and anger doesn't go away quickly. Parents may see obvious jealousy in statements such as "Take it back" or "Couldn't we have a puppy instead?" Parents need to be sensitive to these comments and respond with reassurance.

Jealousy may manifest itself more subtly in regressive behavior, such as whining, sleep disturbances, toileting problems, renewed thumb-sucking, and fear of the dark. Parents must be careful not to view these behaviors as bad but as a call for reassurance. They can help the child by discussing feelings he or she is experiencing.

Some parents give the other children a gift when the new baby comes home; others keep a supply of little gifts on hand and give one to the older child when guests arrive with presents for the baby. It needn't be anything expensive — it's just the idea of receiving and unwrapping a gift that makes them feel appreciated. This need not happen every time a gift is presented to the new baby. Parents should follow their instincts. Also, try letting the older child be in charge of handling and helping open the baby's gifts. Encourage the child to gather toys he hasn't used in the past few months to give to the baby, such as a rattle or ball. Most importantly, parents should consider setting aside special time with the older child to read, cuddle, or go for a ride in the car.

Some children may be afraid to express negative feelings about the baby. The most natural response for children is ambivalence — they like the baby in some ways and they dislike the baby in other ways. They're entitled to both feelings, and it's healthiest if both are expressed. If parents don't observe any negative feelings, the child is probably repressing them.

Parents should make a special effort to adhere to routines during this time. Young children may fear that the baby is taking their place and changing their whole world, so the security of regular routines, especially at bedtime, reassures them and helps them to absorb and integrate the change. Be cautious about overusing the "You're my big girl now" strategy. The older child may need to act like a baby now and then.

Bringing home a new baby will cause younger children a certain amount of pain, no matter what parents do to soften it. Remember that there's a positive side, too. Adjusting to a new baby can be an opportunity for emotional growth in children. Learning to accept another person and to share the love of parents is a valuable experience. A sibling can be a great gift.

PARENTING POINTERS

➤ Children should be permitted to help prepare for the new baby.

➤ Visiting mom and baby in the hospital can be a reassuring experience for siblings.

➤ Parents should anticipate jealousy and possible regressive behavior.

➤ Providing small gifts for the older child can help make the child continue to feel special.

➤ Children are entitled to a range of feelings about the new baby and should be encouraged to talk about them.

➤ Following normal routines, as much as possible, can be comforting to siblings.

21. Reading aloud
A simple way to increase children's reading skills

Most parents recognize the value of good reading skills and are eager for their children to embrace books. Reading is a foundation for learning and achievement in school. But parents may be surprised to learn that reading aloud to their children is the most important factor in determining their child's reading success.

Studies show the benefits of reading aloud are numerous. It builds the child's vocabulary and knowledge base. As for language development, it introduces textures and nuances of English that are rarely heard on TV or in everyday conversation. It establishes the connection between reading and writing in a child's mind and it exposes children to a wealth of experiences beyond their immediate world. Reading also stimulates imagination, stretches short attention spans, and nourishes emotional development in children. And, reading aloud can encourage compassion, reshaping negative attitudes to positive ones. For example, hearing the story of Bambi inspires sympathy for the loss of another. Reading a story about a successful young athlete who overcame obstacles may encourage a child to try an endeavor that he previously thought was too difficult.

A parent's reading aloud is an advertisement for learning to read, which can be overwhelming to a child. This joy of reading can be contagious. A child can sense the enthusiasm of a parent who is reading a story. Just as it is important to teach children how to read, it is important to motivate them to read.

When a child hears good fiction read aloud, he can receive knowledge seemingly above his level. Listening comprehension develops before reading comprehension. For example, a child reading on a second-grade level may be able to listen to books written on a fourth-grade level. The vocabulary he builds while listening will feed his reading vocabulary in the future. When a child hears a new word in the context of a story, he will be likely to figure out its meaning and add it to his overall vocabulary. Then, when he learns to read it, it will be easier for him.

There is a direct link between reading and knowledge. After all, the more you read, the more you know. The more you know, the smarter you grow. By hooking a child on reading, a parent can influence the child's success in school and future career opportunities. Other benefits of reading aloud are not as measurable, but just as important. Parents and children who read together strengthen their relationship as they enjoy the ritual of snuggling up together to share a story.

So, just as parents talk to children well before children learn to talk, they should read to children long before children learn to read. It's almost impossible to read to children too early or too much.

PARENTING POINTERS
➤ Reading aloud is the most important factor in influencing a child's success at reading.

➤ Children can understand and benefit from listening to stories that are beyond their reading level.

➤ By exposing children to new words through reading, they will pick up on vocabulary more quickly as they learn to read.

➤ It is never too early to start reading to a child.

22. Language development
Talking with kids is the key

Simply talking with children is one of the best ways to stimulate language development. But often parents find it's not that easy to talk with young children. When parents try to carry on a conversation with a child, sometimes it just doesn't seem to go anywhere.

Conversation, however, can flow when parents master some basic communication skills. Parents can start by regularly asking their children what they think and what they feel. It is important to show genuine interest. Be a good listener. Children love to be heard and will gradually feel more comfortable about expressing their thoughts.

Parents can encourage a dialogue by asking questions. For example, "What animals did you like best at the zoo?" This requires more than just a yes or no answer or a correct answer, which often leads a conversation to a dead end.

In turn, parents need to share their thoughts with their child. For instance, a parent who is deciding how to rearrange a room can get the child involved with open-ended questions like: "I'm not sure where to put this new shelf. Where do you think would be a good place?" or "If we put it here, then where could we move the bookcase?" Parents may be surprised about the enthusiasm involving children in decisions can create. Kids like to feel that their input is valued and that they're important enough to be consulted.

Sometimes, just reflecting a child's feelings back will encourage her to tell what's on her mind. "You're really sad today, aren't you Lauren?" might be a better question than "What's wrong?" because children may have trouble pinpointing what they're feeling. If something seems to be bothering a child, a parent should make the best guess about what's wrong and phrase a question indirectly. "It's the noise of the hammering that's bothering you, isn't it?" is one approach. If the guess proves correct, the parent should talk with the child about possible solutions, such as finding a quiet corner or stopping the hammering temporarily. If the parent has guessed wrong, the child will clarify what's the matter. In any case, the door to communication has been opened.

Another way to stimulate a child's language development is to extend a conversation that a child is having with someone else. For instance, a parent hears Jenny ask Tommy (who rarely talks) if he watched a Peanuts special last night. Tommy might say no and Jenny walks away. At this point, the parent could ask Tommy, "What do you like to watch on TV?" If he mentions a specific program, talk about why he likes it. Or, talk about other programs he watches, whether he likes to watch with anyone else, what he likes best to do after school, and so on. Parents should watch the child for cues that he has finished talking and be ready to end the conversation.

Through conversation, children can sort out their feelings and learn to express themselves. Once children can articulate their thoughts, it is easier for parents and caregivers to understand and respond to their needs.

PARENTING POINTERS

➤ With a little effort, adults can learn to carry on meaningful conversations with children.

➤ Parents need to express interest in their children's thoughts and opinions.

➤ Open-ended questions can prompt a good conversation.

➤ In a difficult situation parents may get a child to open up by reflecting a child's feelings back to him.

➤ Tune into children's interests and ask questions related to what they are already talking about with others.

23. Death

Reassuring and comforting children through grief

Grief is often accompanied by anger, fear, sorrow, and guilt. Sharing and comforting someone as they move through their many feelings can bring relief. By expressing pain a family can move ahead. It is a group process. Real courage is knowing pain and going on with life. We need to talk with our children to help them grieve and feel the pain.

It is natural for children to ask questions about death as they explore life. The parent's task is to respond in language children can understand, without needlessly frightening them about their own mortality. Although there is no one "right" way to handle this situation, there are basic guidelines that can help make kids feel safe and more durable in the face of loss.

Parents earn trust with the truth. Kids' fantasies are usually worse than reality, and truth can help overcome fears. Parents can share facts about death and dying without offering graphic details. When someone dies, explain that there are severe injuries or illnesses that no medicine or treatment will cure. For example, sometimes the brain becomes damaged and stops working. It is important to assure the child that there was no way to save the person's life.

The scientific fact of death should be clarified so the child knows the dead person is not hurting. For example, tell a child, "There is no thinking or feeling when the body is dead." Explanations that create ghosts or threaten the child's privacy can be scary. "He's always watching you" is difficult for kids to comprehend.

In addition, platitudes can confuse children and generate anxiety and anger. For example, telling a child that the person who has died is "in a better place" may be hard to grasp. Religion can be a source of comfort, but children must grasp the scientific reality of death before they can understand it in the religious context.

It's important to help children prepare for dealing with societal procedures around death. If she chooses to attend the funeral or visit the grave, she needs to know what will be seen and heard there. With the help of a caring parent, a child of any age can go to a viewing. This should be done privately, giving the child a chance to say good-bye in her own way. A parent can use this time to explain why the body is still and why the person may not look the same as when he was alive. Attending the grave site service should be left up to the child.

Parents can help a child work through a grieving process in the days and weeks following the death. Initially children are bewildered and numbed by the loss of a close loved one. They may float through the first few days. After they realize what has actually happened, they may become very anxious about who will take care of them and if they are safe. They may be angry, upset, withdrawn, or depressed.

If the child is successfully helped through this stage, then real mourning will follow. Expect healthy sorrow that ranges from happy to depressed to angry to normal. It comes in waves and may be accompanied by physical complaints or sleep disturbances. The whole grief process can take about two years, depending on the child's age and the intensity of the relationship with the dead person. Remember, every child is an individual and each response will be unique.

Helping children express their grief is the most important thing a parent can do. It's not so much what the child says, but that the parent is willing to listen — often with patience and reassurance — that makes the difference. Grieving children need to know that they aren't grieving alone. They should understand that the family is experiencing the pain together and that the group can support the individual in grief.

PARENTING POINTERS
➤ Being truthful and straightforward with children about death helps them overcome their confusion and fear.

➤ Parents should encourage children to talk about their feelings and concerns.

➤ Children need to be prepared about what to expect at a funeral, grave site or viewing.

➤ Expect children to go through various stages in the grieving process.

➤ Children should be reminded that they are not alone in their grief.

24. Safety and strangers
Preparing children to protect themselves

Parents want children to be friendly and open, yet guarded and safe. Adults also want to be warm and friendly, yet self-protective as well. Yet, with caution and good sense, parents and children can retain their humanity and concern for others while living safely.

Most parents are well versed in teaching their children how to deal with strangers. They work hard to help them differentiate a stranger from a friend. While parents want children to be warm and friendly, children need to learn to keep themselves safe.

Adults, too, have to think about how they should respond when approached by a strange child. In today's world, an adult's overly friendly response to a strange child can be misconstrued by a child's parent as an unwelcome gesture. In both cases, however, common sense and caution can provide a framework of action.

The rules for children dealing with strangers are clear. Parents should repeat all the important adages beginning when the young child is starting to be independent and can understand the concepts. Be alert. Travel with at least one other person. Walk along well-traveled routes and don't take shortcuts. Children need to learn the value of following a routine. Let children know that by traveling home from school using the same route, without diversions or shortcuts, a parent will be able to find them if needed. If the child follows a daily routine, neighbors will become familiar with his patterns and help him find help, if necessary.

Without alarming children about the dangers involved, parents need to be explicit about not getting in a car with anyone, unless the parent has cleared it with the child in advance. As for other adults picking up children, using a code word is helpful. This is especially important in certain divorce or separation situations. For example, if a parent pre-arranges for another adult to pick up a child after school, the adult and child should use an agreed-upon password such as "macaroni" to confirm that the pick up is part of the parent's plan.

Then, there are the old standbys. Children should never take candy or presents from strangers, and never give directions to anyone. If approached by a vehicle, run in the opposite direction, so that the car has to turn around to follow.

Kids need to know they can get help if threatened by running into a nearby house, store, or public place. If physically grabbed, they should scream loudly "Fire!" or "This is not my dad!" A scream alone may be overlooked as a family disagreement.

Adult rules for approaching strange children follow similar cautions. Adults must think, "How can I best protect myself while helping this child?" The best response is to smile and to ask the child if he is lost and who is taking care of him. Then, after a quick look around to see if he is in any distress, redirect him back to the destination or purpose that he shared.

If he is in some obvious distress, an adult should get help immediately. For example, if an adult sees a child who is being dragged through a shopping mall, she should find a security guard to determine what is happening. Because children are naturally inquisitive and trusting, parents must remain vigilant to ensure kids have a safe and memorable childhood.

PARENTING POINTERS

➤ Parents should teach children to be alert, keep to their routines, and avoid temptations from strangers.

➤ When a child is physically threatened, he should seek help and scream something specific such as, "This is not my mom" rather than merely, "No," which may not get attention.

➤ Adults need to be wary of being too friendly with strange children. If uncertain, inquire about what the child needs. If it is an obvious crisis, get help.

25. Sexual stereotyping
Avoiding labels and encouraging individuality

It starts when the baby receives pink or blue clothes; certain expectations are placed on children based on gender. Parents may even catch themselves saying, "That's not lady-like" or "Act like a man." But with the growing awareness of the effect of sexual stereotyping, many parents are trying to avoid the subtle conditioning of their children based on sex. While there is some controversy surrounding this subject, the important thing is for kids to have a balance and to be encouraged to develop all aspects of their personalities.

Most psychologists agree that human beings are a complex mix of strong and weak, hard and soft, and other qualities that we traditionally think of as male and female. Gradually, society is learning to accept both sides of men and women, so it is more acceptable now for women to be assertive and for men to be sensitive.

Part of every parent's job is to prepare their children for real life roles that accept males and females for what they are, not just as the stereotypes that once predominated. For example, a young boy today may need to learn to clean house, cook meals, or care for children to be a productive member of a modern family where both partners share in work at home. Similarly, a girl may play ice hockey, mow the lawn, or become a police officer.

The parent's efforts with young children can start with buying clothes and toys that aren't gender specific. Girls shouldn't always have to wear dresses, especially when pants are more comfortable; boys can enjoy playing with dolls. Both genders should be introduced to as many different stimuli as possible.

As children grow up, parents should become aware of their developing character. Parents can encourage a boy to talk about his feelings and learn to be sensitive, rather than discouraging him from being too aggressive. A boy who learns to be open and caring as a child may grow up to be a sensitive parent and citizen. Likewise with young girls, it's best not to try to eliminate their softer side but, rather, to encourage them to be assertive. For example, if a young girl appears to be giving in quickly when an argument begins, parents can encourage her to voice her opinions more strongly.

Children also need to spend time with adults of both sexes. If there is no father in the home, perhaps a male member of the extended family — an uncle, or a volunteer from the community — can serve as a surrogate father to a young boy or girl.

Most important, parents shouldn't try to force a child into a certain kind of behavior. This almost always backfires. For example, some fathers may be concerned if their sons aren't immediately interested in football, baseball, or other traditional male sports. But traditional sports aren't for everyone. Tennis, track or less-structured physical activities can teach the same valuable lessons of sportsmanship. If pushed too hard, a child may choose not to participate in any activity at all.

Role models and expectations for girls have greatly changed, too. Increased opportunities for women have opened the door of possibilities for girls. Girls need to be motivated to succeed just like boys. If girls are told they can do anything, they will likely take on life with that attitude. Girls, however, shouldn't be pushed to repress any of their traditional "female" behaviors. Girls can be encouraged to develop both their ambitious and nurturing sides. Allowing girls choices and balance is the key.

When there are children of both sexes in the family, the proper balance of behavior can be encouraged by equal treatment. Punishments and rewards do not have to be based on gender alone. For example, allowances or duties around the house should be based on age and ability, not gender.

With some concerted effort parents can help children develop their potential as individuals. By tapping into their own strengths rather than following society's expectations, children mature with the comfort and confidence of being themselves.

PARENTING POINTERS

➤ Parents can help children be prepared for real life roles by encouraging them to develop well-rounded skills, not just those based on stereotypes.

➤ Parents should not push a child into behaving in a way based on gender but, rather, recognize the child's individuality.

➤ To set a good example parents should distribute chores and perks equally among boys and girls in a family.

III

Living with Older Children

26. Friendship
Teaching your child to bond with others

As children grow they become social creatures, keen on making and keeping friends. When they start school, they enter a new social period in their life and become anxious to interact with others outside their family.

It's crushing to kids when their attempts to make friends are rebuffed. This happens to most children from time to time, and sometimes their own actions may have contributed to this problem. If they learn to understand nonverbal communication and be a welcoming friend, they will be more successful as they try to form friendships.

As children interact they may give emotional messages as well as verbal ones. Small changes in facial expressions, gestures, or tone of voice can send inappropriate or negative signals or be misinterpreted by potential friends. Or, a child may not be able to interpret the signals that other children give him in response. Either problem can lead to social rejection.

A child may not understand the facial expressions and gestures of others because she has never been taught to listen and watch carefully. She needs to learn how to pick up on the meaning communicated by someone's tone of voice or body language. In this way, she'll know whether someone is accepting or not. Or, maybe the child doesn't show pleasant, accepting facial expressions that match her desire for friendship.

Some children learn that they can seem more friendly to others if they smile. A child who is nervous may try to be cool and show no expression at all, which can be a turn-off. Other children need to learn the importance of giving the other person their personal space, so they don't stand too close or unwillingly touch the person in an unwelcome way.

Children can visit friends independently as soon as they feel familiar and relaxed in the new surroundings. One suggestion is for parents to arrange a neutral meeting place, such as a local playground, where children can play without worrying about whose toy is whose.

At ages two to three, children engage in playing side by side with other children, but not necessarily interacting because their language skills aren't fully developed. At ages three to four, however, there is an explosion of language development and children begin to play together. They still have to learn to share and parents can demonstrate the process. A parent can show children how to play cooperatively, and encouraging children to share and be kind is important.

For older children, parents can teach them to be flexible about what activity is chosen in play. An example of negotiation may be, "Let's play ball for awhile outside, then I'll paint with you inside." It helps to desensitize kids to any teasing from others. If they feel good about themselves, they can handle any situation with humor and control.

Parents should encourage children to talk about their friendships. Through these discussions, parents can give their children ideas about how to be a good friend. A parent who offers encouragement and suggests coping strategies will prepare a child to make and keep friends throughout his or her life.

PARENTING POINTERS

➤ Children need to learn to tune into the nonverbal signals that they send to potential friends. Something as simple as teaching a child to smile and be friendly can help open doors to friendships.

➤ When arranging play dates, parents might consider a neutral meeting place, such as a park, where it may be easier for kids to share.

➤ Parents can help older children be good friends by acting kind and learning to negotiate.

27. Peer pressure
Learning to stand up to others

At some point, most children will be pressured by peers to do something they normally wouldn't do on their own. This behavior may be dishonest, illegal, or against the child's personal and family values. Temptations during teen years may involve skipping school, shoplifting, using alcohol or drugs, or being sexually active. The child will likely feel torn between knowing what is right, and not wanting to disappoint or lose friends.

Children need to learn effective ways to say "no" to peer pressure. They need to know that it's okay to believe and act differently than their friends. It takes good self-esteem and strong communication skills to stand up to peer pressure. With the support of parents and effective family communication skills, children can succeed in making healthy, independent decisions.

There are several ways a child can respond to peer pressure. First, he can simply be straightforward and blunt. When asked to share answers on a math test he might say, "I can't do that. It's cheating. I don't want to get into trouble." It's difficult for some children to take such a strong stand, however.

Another response may be for a child use her parent as an excuse. Children may actually be relieved when parents establish definite rules and limits, giving them an "out" in the face of pressure. A child can say, "I couldn't possibly do that. My dad says that if I'm not in by 11 o'clock, I'll be in big trouble." It's best for the child to simply state this reason and exit quickly.

A child who is honest with her peers may find an ally among her friends. She may discover that another child in the group feels the same reluctance to participate in a certain activity. Peers often will try to convince her that "everyone does it," so she'll be relieved to know other friends side with her. Bargaining with friends is another way to fend off peer pressure. For instance, in response to pressure to shoplift, a child could say, "If you ask me to steal that, I won't go to the movies with you on Saturday."

It's best for children to state their objections to an unwanted activity directly and decisively. Putting off the decision, or making silly excuses will only prolong the situation. Parents need to remind children that they are individuals who can determine their own actions. In the end, his self-esteem and sense of competence will grow through standing up to peer pressure.

PARENTING POINTERS

➤ By helping build a child's confidence, parents can encourage a child to stand up to peer pressure effectively and directly.

➤ If parents set appropriate limits, a child may welcome using parents as a way to stand up to peers.

➤ Encourage a child to seek out support among friends.

➤ Open communication between parent and child can help give the child a place to turn during difficult times with peers.

28. Drugs
Parental strategies for raising "clean" kids

Although schools are making a concerted effort to educate children about drugs and alcohol, parents still have the greatest impact on their children's behavior. Parents need to be prepared to take responsibility and confront the challenge of raising drug-free kids. As children face a whole new world of drug availability, they need their parents' help more than ever to say no.

First, parents need to educate themselves about current drugs and their effects. Parents don't have to be a walking encyclopedia on drug facts, but they should know the basics. Second, parents should model the behavior of non-use. If they behave as if drugs are the solution to every problem, their children likely will behave the same way. Children are much more prone to use drugs or alcohol if their parents smoke cigarettes, abuse alcohol, use any substance to help lessen stress, or have an ambivalent attitude toward drugs.

Communication is also important. When using prescription drugs, parents should explain to their children the medicine's purpose. When using alcohol, tell children that it is a beverage that responsible adults can choose to use. Kids learn best by example, so parents need to be consistent in their attitudes about drinking or drugs. It won't help children to let them drink on occasion at home with the rationalization that, "I'd rather them drink at home than out on the street." It's still giving approval to illegal substance abuse, and it could lead to future addiction.

There are various reasons kids use drugs, and there are parental strategies to counteract each one. For example, since peer pressure most often leads to teenage drinking, parents should work to build up their child's self-esteem and confidence. Parents can do this by encouraging the child's positive interests and individuality. Parents should also monitor and guide their child's friendships and get to know the parents of their child's friends.

Teens may use drugs and alcohol out of a sense of boredom and hopelessness. To counteract this, parents can expose their kids to as many interests as possible and provide a constructive home environment. Studies suggest that television dependence can be transferred to substance dependence, so monitoring the amount of TV time can help.

Some kids do drugs simply to escape the stress of their life — competitive sports, personal relationships, or school difficulties. Parents can teach that hardships are just as much a part of life as good fortune. Kids need to know that when the burden seems too great, they can turn to their parents, family and friends for support. Emphasize that drugs and alcohol offer only temporary relief from pain. Parents can encourage non-competitive, satisfying activities as an alternative relief from stress, such as music or art.

Teenagers often associate maturity with smoking, drinking, and drug use. Parents can help children feel grown-up in other more positive ways. Let kids make informed decisions about matters that affect them, such as clothing, meals, or decorating. As children grow up, parents can increase their responsibilities and privileges, too.

Finally, many people take drugs because they make them feel good, and kids are no exception. Drugs may produce a fleeting euphoria, but kids need to understand that there are other ways to feel good that don't have the dangerous side-effects. Parents can combat this by making home a real haven where children receive love, support and advice. With open communication and modeling, parents have a great chance to succeed in raising drug-free kids.

Parents should teach kids healthy decision-making and refusal skills. Keep in mind that it's hard for kids to say no because the offer generally comes from friends, not strangers. Teach them the words to use when saying no, then let them practice using the words. It's important to teach these skills early, because waiting until the situation arises means the child has to make a very important life decision with great peer pressure.

In making a difficult decision, kids should identify the problem, list all the options, and review the possible outcomes of each. Then, he can select the best option and act on his decision. When he knows to refuse, he should just say "no"— a firm but friendly "no thanks" or "not today."

PARENTING POINTERS

➤ To be most effective in discussing drugs with kids, parents should learn about the current drug scene.

➤ Parents need to serve as role models, avoiding drug use, smoking, and excessive drinking.

➤ Children use drugs for a variety of reasons, including boredom and stress. Talk with kids about alternative, less destructive ways to cope with life's challenges.

➤ A loving, supportive home environment can give kids a haven from the tempting world of drugs.

29. Pre-adolescence
Tuning in to a child's changes

When children begin to try on the role of being an adult, they've entered pre-adolescence. This usually occurs between the ages of nine and ten and lasts until age 12 or 13. Pre-adolescence is the stage prior to puberty, before physical sexual characteristics have developed. Girls experience rapid physical growth during this time, while boys have growth spurts after puberty.

Parents may have a hard time recognizing subtle changes in their child at this age. The child probably has mastered many skills and fits in well at home, in school, and with friends. He seems to accept parental values, carries out his own responsibilities at home, and likes doing activities as a family. However, he may begin to show irritation with younger siblings in the six-to-nine-year range. Then other signs of restlessness may start to appear.

Pre-adolescents start to be concerned about their bodies and sexual activity. Girls may be worried about approaching menstruation. Teaching children to respect and value their bodies in an ongoing process. It can begin whenever children bring up questions, but the answers should be appropriate for the child's emotional and physical maturity. Parents should start talking more specifically to their children about their pending sexual development around the age of nine or ten. The exact timing depends on the emotional maturity of the child and the stage of physical maturity. There is some benefit, however, in starting before they actually enter puberty because the children won't take the information personally, and it will be easier to expand on these conversations later.

By age 11 or 12 youngsters become very restless. They may develop odd gestures and mannerisms such as facial tics, jerky movements, or speech disorders, such as stuttering. There is also an increased pressure to be exactly the same as peer group members. For example, kids may start being concerned about wearing the right clothes or being involved in activities that are considered popular. Pre-adolescents often have cursory interest in the opposite sex, expressing their interest by badgering or annoying someone.

Children at this stage of development may become distrustful and irritated with their parents. Parents will often hear their children say in exasperation, "You just don't understand." All of a sudden, your compliant child may not want to obey the same rules that didn't seem to be a problem a year ago. Children may also object to keeping clean and dressing appropriately. There is a heightened sensitivity to privacy and increased dissatisfaction with their bodies.

Basically, pre-adolescents are confronted with two major tasks. First, they must shed their childhood personalities, which are typically more adherent to rules and structure, as they confront the more adult world of making choices and not following parental dictates. Children's minds are set on rules and what's fair. As pre-adolescents, they become disorganized and have difficulty maintaining this conformity as they become individuals. Secondly, they must also begin to identify more with peers and pull away from parents. Peers may prompt a pre-adolescent to wear sophisticated clothing, to use profanity, or get poor grades.

Parents should be sensitive to the fact that an outwardly confident pre-adolescent may have moments of being scared and overwhelmed. It's not easy to have to struggle against the people on whom he depends and loves. Parents should let their child know that it is all right to feel unsure at times, and that it is important to communicate needs and feelings.

Pre-adolescence can be threatening for parents, too. The child's emotional swings, such as maintaining attachments for old stuffed animals at one moment and having a superior attitude the next can be unnerving. Parents miss the cooperative and friendly ten-year-old, and they begin to question their parenting skills. They may respond with mistrust and stricter rules, which only invites counter-attacks and rebellion.

Pre-adolescence is a time of uncertainty for both the parent and child. It's reassuring to note that in not too many years the pre-adolescent will have become an independent, responsible person.

PARENTING POINTERS

➤ Although a pre-adolescent may become dramatic at times, it is important for the parent to remain calm.

➤ Parents should look for the real meaning behind the struggles with their children at this age. Remember to choose the battles worth fighting.

➤ Pre-adolescents are searching for adventure in their lives. Parents can provide a lifestyle that allows for growth and discovery.

➤ Parents need to treat pre-teens sensitively. For example, a pre-adolescent probably doesn't want to be called a child or reprimanded in public.

30. Adolescence
Strategies to help children discover themselves

Adolescence is a difficult time for every family member. Relationships between parents and children can become strained and volatile during this intense period of change. Adolescents begin rejecting, challenging, and judging parents and, as a result, even the most secure parent can begin to question his or her parenting skills. Parents need to prepare themselves for the adolescent years by understanding what is normal teen behavior and incorporating strategies to deal with it.

Adolescents are between childhood and adulthood. This occurs after puberty until the time that kids able to manage their own lives. Some of the milestones beyond the physical changes include a pulling back from family as children become more autonomous and developing more friendships with the opposite sex.

The classic "I" and "M" describe normal teen behavior. The "I" stands for impulsive, intense, idealistic, immediate, (meaning they want everything right now), and impervious (they think that nothing can hurt them). The "M" relates to moody, messy, monosyllabic, mouthy, money-oriented, and me-centered. Although these characteristics may try parents' patience, they are necessary for any teen's primary work: establishing a clear identity and his/her own beliefs and values; achieving emotional independence from parents and creating friendships with friends of both sexes; making a commitment to his future by beginning to choose a career and the type of mate he would prefer. These are tough tasks for a young person to face.

Teens are worried about their body image and sexual identity too.
Adolescence often is marked by excessive modesty, insecurity, and a concern with how others perceive the adolescent, as teens deal with the issue of self-acceptance. Girls typically go through the physical changes at an earlier age than boys.

Teenagers may be idealistic and have strong opinions about politics and religion, which can spark highly spirited family dialogues. They are naturally self-centered, but because they want independence above all, they can't help but question parental values and they often turn to peers for direction and acceptance. Adolescence is an age of extreme physical growth, with hormonal upheavals. This can contribute to poor judgment and bad decisions. Adolescents may do things they would never do as adults, acting out behaviors in ways that ultimately teach them what they don't want to be.

Dangers abound at this stage, particularly in the areas of drug and alcohol, and sexual activity. Adolescents who are over-involved in sex or abuse alcohol are at a higher risk for suicide. They need to hear the facts about birth control and drug addiction. Adolescents may believe idealistically that there is but one true love for everyone, so break-ups with their first loves may be painful and traumatic. They need to hear from adults that this is not their last chance.

Parents can help teens through adolescence by acknowledging "rites of passage" and attaching certain privileges to an age or achievement. Talk with teens about setting life goals, acknowledging, however, that goals may change. While not giving teens total freedom, parents should offer less restrictions as teens grow older and show they can be trusted.

As a teen navigates the passage to adulthood, his parents can help him control impulses and regulate his need for excitement, while giving him privacy and respect as an individual. Basically, parents should loosen their grip in certain areas while tightening it on the most important issues such as safety, since teens feel invincible to danger. Parents must be careful not to match the level of emotional intensity of their teen. Remaining calm and offering simple, clear consequences for misbehavior is best.

Teens also need to know when they've done a good job, although they may seem unreceptive and uncommunicative at times. Teens should feel that despite the fickleness of friendships and the world outside, they are accepted, loved, and safe at home.

PARENTING POINTERS

➤ Parents should to be available to their adolescent, offering direction but not too much control.

➤ In today's society, parents need to talk frankly with teens about drugs and birth control.

➤ Parents need to let their teen know that no matter what he does they will always be there for him. Although the parents may not like a behavior, they will always love him.

31. The super kid
Guidance for avoiding stressed-out children

In this increasingly fast-paced world, adults try to balance the pressures of demanding jobs, married life, and social obligations, while trying to squeeze in leisure time activities. This can create a climate of stress and intense expectations. As adults hurry to keep up with the lives they've created, they pay a price for maintaining this pace. No one pays a higher price, however, than children who often are being rushed into adulthood trying to meet our high expectations.

A "super kid" is a child who is pushed by parents at a very early age to learn, compete, and achieve. The wunderkind is becoming an alarmingly common part of today's competitive society. She is being taught to read at a remarkably early age, and is being shuttled from one activity to another, learning everything from art to soccer. With all this structured activity, there is little time is left for carefree play and relaxation.

This hectic pace for children can have serious consequences. Super kids may think that their parents primarily value them for their achievements and performances. Some children become over-achievers by pouring all of their energy into meeting their parents' expectations. As a result, they miss out on important opportunities for social or emotional growth. On the other hand, the anger and anxiety resulting from parental expectations can have the opposite effect. For example, children may deliberately perform poorly in school. Their bottled-up aggression may come out in their relationships with peers. A bad self-image could cause them to become withdrawn.

How can parents prevent their children from experiencing this kind of stress? It's a matter of attitude. Parents must pay attention to the child's emotional needs and help her develop at her own pace. This also has the added benefit of slowing things down for the parents, too.

Free and unstructured play is essential to any child's emotional and social growth. This is how children practice living skills and try on different roles. They need time to talk to butterflies, daydream, and "hang out." Play gives them a chance to grow and learn in vital ways.

Parents should help children through each stage of development with structure and motivation that is appropriate to the child's age. By staying focused on the child's present age and not pressuring the child to consider future challenges too soon, parents can prevent stress. For example, rather than expressing excessive concern about the reading ability of a kindergarten child, a parent can help him with the real tasks of that developmental age—discovering who he is and moving beyond the boundaries of home and family. Together the parent and child should explore the child's capacities, strengths, and limits.

The issue of the super kid often is really about the super mom or super dad. Parents should question the motivations behind their expectations and not try to live their lives through their children. Be more concerned with the child's basic health and happiness than any super achievement.

Children who are given the freedom to be uniquely themselves can move into society with a sense of competence. When children feel good about themselves, the possibilities for true achievement are limitless.

PARENTING POINTERS

➤ Parents need to focus on age-appropriate activities and expectations for their child.

➤ It's important for children to have down time to relax and just play.

➤ Parents should assess their own motivation behind their child's involvement in activities. Be sure that it is the child who wants to participate, not just the parent who is trying to be a "super mom" or "super dad."

32. Co-curricular activities
Arriving at the right balance

By participating in co-curricular or extra-curricular activities, children can make friends, discover new talents, and have fun. They can learn important lessons through sports and clubs that they may not otherwise develop in the structure of school or home. Whether it's playing on a soccer team or singing in the chorus, activities provide an opportunity for kids to develop peer relationships. They also can acquire new skills, such as athletic coordination or artistic technique. Developing a talent can build a child's self-esteem.

Both parents and children must make choices about how, where, and with whom they'll spend their time. Opportunities to get involved abound. When choosing an extra-curricular activity the family needs to consider its finances, time, and energy level required by the child. As enthusiastic as kids might be about signing up for a new activity, parents need to be realistic about the energy that will be required of the entire family to keep up. In addition to escorting children to activities, balancing a job and the demands of home can be stressful. This is especially true for single parents, or families where one spouse travels frequently. A good coping strategy might be to form networks with other families to combine resources that allow you to carpool or share meals.

When determining what activities are best, remember that children are easily over-stimulated. One activity may be enough, especially for young children. Parents might suggest two activities that fit into the family's schedule and budget and let the child choose. Older children can handle several activities, but they still need some unstructured time. If children are constantly engaged in organized activities, they miss the chance to learn to play alone or develop creativity. Also, parents need to monitor whether children's activities become so demanding that they interfere with school work, which needs to be a priority. This does not mean that it's necessary to stop activities altogether, since many children benefit from success in areas outside of school. Just make an adjustment to the amount of time spent at any particular activity. The key is to maintain a balance in your child's life.

Parents should respect that their child's needs and interests may be different than their own. Don't be overly concerned if a child starts an activity, then loses interest. A child may decide to quit an activity if he discovers it's not for him. However, be sure that he gives it a fair chance. Encourage him to stick with it. It may just be a question of self-confidence and discovering that he can succeed. If it doesn't work out allow him to quit the activity with the suggestion that the child explore the activity at a later time. Children need the freedom to explore their talents and grow in a supportive environment.

PARENTING POINTERS

➤ Involvement in extra-curricular activities can help kids grow in new ways.

➤ Families should consider time, money, and energy when signing up a child for an outside activity.

➤ Children's involvement should be limited, based on their age and maturity.

➤ Parents should expect children's interests to change. Allow kids to quit or switch activities after they give it a good try.

33. Report cards
Keeping perspective on grades

Parents and children know the feeling of anticipation — and sometimes dread — of opening report cards. For children, grades can trigger feelings ranging from pride to rejection. Parents experience similar feelings, for they often view the child's success or failure as evidence of their own parenting skills. Yet, no matter what the grade, parents should try to respond to children in a positive, encouraging manner.

First, grades need to be kept in perspective. Grades and report cards indicate a child's performance in academic and social tasks; they are not moral judgments about the child. Parents should be careful not to correlate bad grades with bad behavior and vice versa. Unfortunately, grades have become so central in education that it's hard to remember they're merely a measuring tool to help decipher a child's progress.

When evaluating how a child is doing, a parent should ask, "Is he performing at grade level?" "Is he on track developmentally?" If the answer is yes, then praise the child for the accomplishment with a comment such as, "You must be proud of yourself." Help him feel proud of what he does accomplish so he'll feel good about it and want to repeat successes. The thinking here is that children need to be motivated to excel for themselves, not to please parents. Good grades should be their own reward. That's why paying for grades is not effective; the grade itself is the payoff and the recognition of the child's hard work.

When a child is having difficulty in school, parents need to get involved and find out how to help. It's not a good idea to punish or demean the child, nor is it wise to assume responsibility for his learning. Parents should identify the problem, then discover ways to help without taking over the situation. Talk with the teacher to find out if the child is putting forth his best effort. Good communication with the teacher creates an environment where the child can succeed. The teacher can get to understand the child's needs and the parent can be the child's advocate and support the teacher's efforts.

Restricting privileges, such as watching television, is appropriate when grades are unacceptable. Some children need a certain structure and limits to succeed. Not all children are self-motivating, so parents can help by setting priorities and limits. Parents can then negotiate with the child what needs to be done to reinstate the privilege.

Parents can encourage a child by showing interest in what she's doing in school. At the dinner table, ask the child open-ended questions what she is learning in school. Parents can also model reading and an interest in academic pursuits. Reading aloud to children helps them become better readers.

It's important to make the arrival of the report card a positive time of discussion and reflection. First, review the report card with the child and discuss what it means. The conversation alone may help the child make changes, if necessary, in how he approaches his schoolwork.

Parents should refrain from overreacting or getting angry if the grades aren't up to par. Whether the child shows it or not, he is disappointed and needs parental support. A parent can start the dialogue with, "Let's talk about this." "What do you think is the problem here?" "Would you like me to help you think of some ideas or make a plan?" The parent's role is to offer the child hope and the possibility of improvement; not to punish or lecture or to remove responsibility for academic achievement.

Remember that grades are only one indicator of a child's success in school. Verbal communication with the teacher will supply more details of the child's progress and pinpoint areas to focus on for improvement.

PARENTING POINTERS

➤ Parents need to keep grades and report cards in perspective; they are one way of reporting our children's academic strengths and concerns.

➤ Grades are not a reflection of a child's character or our worth as parents.

➤ Offer hope, support, coaching, and set limits when necessary.

➤ Parents should let the child realize that he is responsible for his own grades. However, parents are available for support and guidance.

34. Stress and the teenager
Successfully handling common pressures

Most teens are in a transitional stage — still mastering stresses from childhood, handling the new stresses of adolescence, and anticipating the pressures of adulthood. This can be both exciting and overwhelming. Here are what some teens have expressed as causing stress in their lives:

"Too many people expect too much from me."

"Sometimes life is too much to take … getting up at 6 a.m. to study for tests, competing in gymnastics, and practicing piano."

"I feel lonely and depressed, and I'm always fighting with my parents."

"I'm afraid of failing."

"It's hard to keep up with everything I'm supposed to do."

Parents can help by teaching their children how to cope with the normal stress of life, and eliminate sources of excess stress. They are also in the position to help teens recognize when they are too stressed and need help. Parents can begin by helping their teens identify stressors in their lives. Pressures may include homework, peer issues, social acceptance, parental pressure, personal appearance, sexual activity and orientation, as well as temptations to use drugs and alcohol.

Stress can come from external sources, such as parents, teachers and society. Teenagers also place expectations on themselves that can cause stress. It's when expectations of teens and others clash that they feel the most overwhelmed. For example, when dad expects a son to be a lawyer, but the boy can only imagine being an artist, this causes stress on both sides.

Parents can help by recognizing and validating these sources of stress. Just saying, "Don't worry, it's just part of growing up" doesn't help. Teens need to hear instead, "I understand that you're stressed about this, so let's talk about what you might do to make it better." Another approach might be, "Looks like you're upset. What's making you angry?"

After parents understand the teen's concerns they can often help by sharing their own life experiences and offering options about how to handle the situation. Be sure to choose the right time to talk, when the teenager is relaxed and open to feedback. Yet, do not let the teen avoid the discussion by saying "not now." When this happens ask when a good time would be and plan an agreed upon time to talk.

When a parent is aware of a teenager's concerns, the parent can anticipate upcoming events that might be stressful and talk about it. For example, a high school student who is about to take the SAT will be less stressed if a parent encourages him to talk about his anxiety in advance. Then he learns to act upon the stress and gain control of the situation, rather than just react when it occurs.

Parents can also help teens decide when their stress has reached an unhealthy level. If a teen is exhibiting any of the following symptoms, he/she may be on overload:

- Sleeping all the time, or not sleeping enough.
- Overeating or undereating.
- Experiencing trouble in school.
- Withdrawing from friends and family.
- Feeling restless, anxious, or depressed.
- Overdoing one thing (too much TV, music or studying).

If any of these situations exist, talk to your teen and let him know he is not alone. Brainstorm about ways to reduce the stress and regain his self-confidence. Communication and mutual understanding help to relieve stress. Making a plan to accomplish tasks is another way to relieve time-related stress.

One goal of every parent is to teach his child to handle things on her own. Learning to deal with stress together not only achieves this

goal of self-reliance, but also brings parents and kids closer in the
transition to a new life-long partnership.

PARENTING POINTERS

➤ Parents can help kids identify and eliminate sources of stress.

➤ Talking through difficult situations can help teens find ways to cope with the pressures of growing up.

➤ Making expectations clear and understanding a teen's perspective can help reduce stress.

➤ Planning and scheduling tasks together can help teens stay organized and not get too overwhelmed.

➤ While some stress is normal during teenage years, parents should be aware of signs of overload and be ready to help the child regain balance in life.

35. Latch-key children
Establishing routines and rules to make it work

By the year 2000 it is estimated that ten million children between the ages of five and 13 will be "latch-key" children. With after-school care often unavailable, inaccessible, or unaffordable, many kids take care of themselves from the time school is out until their parents arrive home.

Leaving a child alone a portion of every day is a source of worry, fear and frustration for many parents. When the situation is not working well, it can be distracting and even job-threatening for parents. Here are some strategies for making the latch-key option more manageable.

A parent needs to assess whether a child is mature enough to take care of herself. Prior to age 11 most children are not ready to be on their own. They have difficulty handling unexpected situations. After age 11 consider whether the child can follow instructions and act responsibly. In making a decision, parents can ask the following questions:

- How mature is my child?
- How excited is the child about staying home alone?
- Is crime a problem in the neighborhood?
- Can the child call a parent at work?
- Can we count on help from neighbors and nearby family?
- Is the child easily scared?
- If necessary, can the child handle the responsibility of preparing meals?

When beginning self-care, the child needs some experience in taking responsibility for himself for short periods, knowing where the parent can be reached. Time alone can increase as the child feels more comfortable. Communication is crucial. Parents need to listen to the child's fears and reservations or his excitement and anticipation about self-care. Remain open to questions and comments about how it feels to be "all alone." Sometimes the routine can be adjusted to make the child feel more comfortable.

Parents can take steps to make the situation work with careful planning and setting expectations. Establish rules that the child can understand and consistently follow. Have a well-developed routine. This might include calling a parent, changing clothes, having a snack, relaxing, doing chores and homework. An after-school routine worked out in advance between parent and child helps the child experience the parent's presence even when not there.

Teach a child to deal with an emergency. A family may rehearse different scenarios and have the child show how she would react. For example, have the child demonstrate how to answer the door. Teach the child how to dial 911 in case of a fire. Explain how to use the first-aid kit for small scrapes and when to call for more help if the situation is more severe.

Checking in with the child by phone can be reassuring, but parents also need to establish a reliable back-up system. Ask neighbors, friends, or relatives to be available to the child — not just in an emergency, but when the child is feeling lonely or scared. Provide the child with the list of people to call if the parent cannot be reached.

When parents come home from work, ten minutes spent just being with the child can be reassuring for both parent and child. The child can share his experience of being at home alone, and be encouraged and praised for doing a good job. A latch-key situation is not ideal, but with planning and a solid routine it can work.

PARENTING POINTERS

➤ Assess the maturity of a child before determining if she can take care of herself after school.

➤ Well-established rules and routines can help the child feel secure while alone. Set clear expectations and rules.

➤ Parents and kids should practice handling emergencies.

➤ Network with neighbors and other family members to provide additional back-up support to the child as needed.

➤ Encourage a child to communicate her concerns or fears about staying home alone and try to modify the routine to make the child feel more comfortable.

36. The gifted child
Supporting the unique child

A wise parent once said, "I know my child is gifted, but he is first of all a child." Parents need to recognize any child's need for play and outdoor exercise, for creative activities and relationships with other children, as well as for intellectual opportunities. But how does a parent know if his child is gifted?

From their early years truly gifted children may demonstrate superior ability — in memory, alertness, or insatiable curiosity. They may indicate an early interest in words and reading, an ability to put two and two together, or show their precocity in learning to walk and talk. A gifted child is usually physically well-developed and socially responsive. She seems to amuse herself and persist in activities longer than the average child of her age. Or, perhaps she has an unusual affinity for music, creating her own combinations and responding intensely to classical music. Being gifted may or may not be tied to an IQ score given to place children in certain programs at school. It has more to do with the child's need for "more" to keep him engaged and productive.

Intelligence is not given once and for all at birth; it develops in response to stimuli in the environment and within the individual. Therefore, exceptional brightness may show up at later times. By providing many opportunities for growth and learning, parents can help their child maximize his potential and grow according to his own schedule, sometimes by leaps and bounds as his mind develops.

Under favorable conditions a gifted child learns readily at school. Parents might talk to the child's teacher about ideas to challenge the child with reading or other interests so that she doesn't become bored and disillusioned with materials that are too easy. The gifted child will probably learn quickly, see relationships, develop superior language ability, solve practical problems, and deal effectively with abstract ideas. But no parent can expect a child to be perpetually active intellectually any more than a physically competent child should be constantly physically active.

Children need time for emotional development as well, and gifted children often progress more slowly in emotional than in intellectual development. Children will usually progress socially at a normal rate, although this may be slower than their intellectual advancements. In mechanical things, too, a gifted child may become impatient with his relatively slower progress. Parents should recognize that a bright child has emotional, social, and physical needs, just as other children do.

Like other children, gifted children need their parents' loving care. They also need reasonable but firm limits to protect them and to strengthen their self-control. Parents should be nurturing and supportive of their children, and not be primarily concerned with their achievements. Gifted children often sense that they're not loved for themselves, but for their performance or achievements. Parents should also try not to label the child as "gifted" so that the child tries to hide it to appear normal.

Parents can help their gifted child most by providing an environment rich in stimuli, learning opportunities and materials, and affection. The child needs freedom to explore, experiment, read, and entertain friends. She needs many outlets for her intellectual interests, but she should not be pushed. Too much pressure may encourage the child to resist learning all together. Parents should let the child take the initiative in using his environment to learn. The parents' role is to give encouragement and appreciate their child's successes, so the entire family enjoys learning together.

PARENTING POINTERS
➤ Parents of gifted children need to encourage a balance of activities to give their child a range of experiences.

➤ It is important that a gifted child feel loved for herself, rather than her talents.

➤ Parents should provide a stimulating, affectionate home environment that gives a child opportunities to learn without pressure.

37. Moving
Preparing kids for a new home, neighborhood, and friends

In our mobile and increasingly global society families often have to relocate. Parents are naturally concerned about the effect a move may have on children. While leaving an old neighborhood and establishing a family in a new home is never easy, there are ways to make it a satisfying transition for everyone.

An important factor is the attitude the parents exhibit toward the move. This will often influence how their children view the change. If parents have a difficult time adjusting to a move, it is obvious to the rest of the family. The process of moving invariably leads to complaints and anxieties. However, the stress can be more manageable if parents talk with the children about the big picture of living in a new house and neighborhood, not just the hassles of moving. Some of the tension can be alleviated by just listening to the kids' concerns and reassuring them that everything will work out.

If there is a decision to be made about whether to move at all, the children can be asked for their input. Options such as having an older child stay with friends or relatives to finish the school year may be possible. Children can be included in discussions but need to know that mom and dad will make the final decision.

Discussing in detail all the concrete aspects of the coming adventure — showing kids the new house, describing the new neighborhood — can make the move exciting. Each family member may have mixed feelings of loss and anticipation. Children should know that their feelings, both good and bad, are normal and healthy.

"I'm going to be all alone and no one will like me" is a common cry of kids not looking forward to moving. Parents can reassure them that they will still be there to help out. Their family won't change just because their neighborhood changes. "We're all in this together as a family" helps, or in cases where one parent is leaving because of divorce or separation, "I'll still be here with you" is a reassurance.

Keeping the routine of family life is very important. Children need predictability and stability in their lives. They want to keep the rules and the structure from their earlier home, especially if there is a separation of the parents or if other aspects of family life change. Stressing the positive side of the move — "Daddy or mommy got a better job and there will be more opportunities for all of us" — increases the anticipation. When there are negative reasons for the move, such as a loss of income or separation, parents can reassure their kids that they will all survive and grow as a family.

Very young children have anxieties that parents take for granted. "Will the truck get there?" "What if my bear is lost?" Let younger children carry their favorite toys with them. Saying something, such as, "We'll have a lot of the same things in our new home" helps young children who think that objects might disappear. Parents should reassure younger children that a pet is coming, or being honest about why a favorite pet has to be left behind.

To older children, friends are central to their lives. Parents can try to find out in advance if there are any other families nearby with kids the same age. Encourage older kids to see a move as a chance to build relationships and develop new strengths. Parents need to recognize and accept an adolescent's possible grief over a move.

The new school is often the scariest part of the move. If children visit the building when it's empty, it's less intimidating on the first day. Walking the route to school before that first day also alleviates a lot of fear, and parents can keep an eye out for children of the same age along the way. If a child, often a young teenager, is very reluctant to move, parents should contact the new guidance counselor or teachers at the school to inform them. Making connection with a local church youth leader may also help. Something to look forward to, such as a new phone that is just theirs, can help ease the transition.

On moving day, including the children in the moving and letting them watch the movers at work keeps them excited about the adventure. The whole family can then take time to have a real good-bye, walking around the neighborhood, throwing a going away party, and taking pictures of people and things to be remembered.

All grief is resolved in time, and children can be more adaptable to change than their parents. Sometimes loneliness is worst at bedtime, so this is a good time to talk about feelings and discoveries. For instance, "New houses have a whole new set of noises — what do they mean?" When children fall into "I miss..." conversations, it helps to acknowledge their feelings and let them cry if they wish. Then say, "Yes, we had some good times there. Remember when we..." It takes time, but anger and disappointment fade, and new experiences become more exciting every day.

PARENTING POINTERS

➤ Including children in the details of moving — touring the new house and neighborhood — can help build excitement and anticipation.

➤ Children need to follow routines as much as possible during the transition of moving.

➤ To minimize the anxiety on the first day of school, parents should try to arrange a tour of a school ahead of time and walk or drive the route to school with kids.

➤ Parents should expect children to miss their old neighborhood and friends for awhile. Encouraging kids to talk about their feelings can help.

38. A new school
Planning and communication help kids adjust

Entering a new school can be one of the most significant transitions in a child's life. Milestones occur when a child starts kindergarten, first grade, middle school, and high school. Other times of transition occur when a child moves to a new district or changes from a primary-level classroom (K-3) to an intermediate environment (grades 4-5). If parents take the lead with planning and communicating, kids can successfully adjust to these new situations.

One of the most difficult adjustments is often entering first grade, when the child may be first encountering a full day at school. The other big jump is into middle school, when the child faces a larger student population of kids from several elementary schools.

Parents can start preparing a child for a new school environment by talking to him about what to expect. Help him visualize how he will get to school, what the classroom will look like, and how the lunch routine will work. Ask the child what he thinks might be different from last year's experience. Through this discussion, the parent may be able to pinpoint anxieties. For example, a child who is anxious about having more homework in middle school may feel better if he and his parent use a daily calendar to help him keep track of his assignments and the parents remind the child that teachers are always available for help before and after school.

In addition, parents need to acknowledge the child's fear of the unknown. You might say, "I can understand you're concerned about this new experience. Tell me what you think it might be like." Validating his concerns allows the child to advance to the next critical step — planning. Planning for the first days of school will remove the mystery. Talk with the child about catching the bus, meeting friends, what to do if a locker gets jammed, or what to do if he is late for class. Parents can help with the transition by meeting key figures at the new school, such as the homeroom teacher or guidance counselor. Inquire about an orientation visit for the parent and student at the school and ask questions about routines and procedures.

If the child is moving to a new school district, register early to alleviate first day confusion. Learn about any differences in curriculum and reassure the child about the changes to expect. Some schools may offer a buddy system or program for new students to help ease the child's transition.

Kids need to know that they are not alone during these significant times of change. By practicing routines and discussing how to get around in a new school, children can feel confident and secure. If parents continue to express interest and support as the child adjusts to his new school, the transition will likely be successful.

PARENTING POINTERS

➤ As a child enters a new school, parents can help him prepare by talking about what to expect.

➤ Reassure a child that it is okay to feel apprehensive going to a new school, but he is not alone during this time of change.

➤ The child and parents should participate in school orientations or arrange for a school tour so the child can feel comfortable on the first day.

➤ Parents should remain tuned into a child's daily concerns and provide continuing support throughout the transition.

IV

Management and Discipline for a Peaceful Home

39. Rules

How to set reasonable limits at home

Teaching children to follow reasonable rules at home is a critical part of responsible parenting. Parents who teach limits to their children are ultimately preparing them to function in society with its many laws and customs. If a child has no limits in the home, it's far more difficult for her to understand the regulations and restrictions of the larger world.

Setting limits means being very clear about what is expected from your child and being equally clear about what the consequences will be if the child doesn't comply. Children younger than two generally don't have the verbal skills to understand the concept of rules. But after age two, children become increasingly more articulate and begin to grasp the principle of cause and effect.

For example, a parent can often get a two- or three-year-old child to cooperate by explaining that if the child does one thing, then another thing will happen. You might say, "If you help me pick up the blocks, we'll go outside and play in the sand." If the result is something that the child wants enough, then compliance comes easily. On the other hand, the consequence might be unpleasant. For example, "If you take your sister's toys, you'll have to go to your room for ten minutes." Therefore, for the best chance of success parents should try to phrase requests in positive terms.

In addition to setting limits for children, parents need to establish consistent rules: The punishment or reward needs to be the same each time. Parents should respond immediately and calmly to the behavior. It is tough for parents who may be exasperated as children learn to control themselves. Still, the most powerful tool parents have is their behavior as an example. If parents engage in a tantrum, children will learn to do the same.

When setting rules, parental expectations need to match the developmental level of the child. A child of three isn't really able to clean up all his toys, but he can do a few small tasks such as putting books back on the shelf and blocks in a box. Likewise, small children can't always control their emotions enough to squelch their anger, but they can be taught that there are more acceptable ways to express feelings than hitting.

So, what kinds of success can parents expect when they begin to establish limits and rules in their home? Initially, parents should expect that it will take time for a child to learn to obey new rules. Children need to be reminded often about household rules and limits. There will be occasional regressions, too. Parents should try to take them in stride — kids really do forget. It may take years before a desirable rule becomes automatic to a child.

Children also tend to be more cooperative to household rules when positive rewards are offered for their good behavior, than when punishments are threatened for negative behavior. And, when the child's motivation to comply is out of love for the parents and a wish for approval, the results are better and more long lasting than if the good behavior is based on fear. Children need to hear when they do well and receive positive affirmations that build their self-esteem. Positive reinforcement motivates better and creates a more loving and calm atmosphere in the home.

PARENTING POINTERS

➤ Parents should tell children very clearly what the limits and expectations are in the household.

➤ Rules need to be consistent, as do rewards and punishments.

➤ Parents should try to be calm when disciplining children.

➤ Children are more likely to respond when positive rewards are offered, rather than to threats for negative behavior.

40. Changing behavior
Consistency and modeling are key

One of the greatest responsibilities and challenges of parenting is to help kids change inappropriate behavior. Whether it's teaching a toddler not to throw a book or reminding a teenager not to miss a curfew, parents continually are trying to modify children's behavior. There are strategies parents can learn to effectively direct change with consistency and patience.

Before attempting to change a child's behavior, parents need to be sure that the change is appropriate. Given the child's developmental and emotional age, it may be helpful for parents to ask themselves, "Why do I need or want this change in my child's behavior?" and "Is this the right time to expect this?"

If the change is appropriate, parents should be very clear with their children about the behavior expected. State what is expected of the child in a calm tone of voice. The parent needs to convey to the child confidence in the child's ability to meet these expectations. It's often difficult for children to correct themselves, so it helps to know that someone believes that they can do it. For example, a parent may say, "I know you can act like a big girl and sit in your chair at the restaurant."

Parents are the primary role models for their children. Therefore, if parents want their kids to act in a certain way, they must set the example. Children aren't as likely to respond to a request that appears to be contrary to what the parent would do. A parent who loses her temper and yells to get her child's attention will have a tough time trying to calm down a screaming, out-of-control child.

Lastly, parents will find it helpful to ignore behaviors that don't hurt their child, others, or any property. Of course, ignoring annoying behaviors isn't always easy, so it's important to put that behavior in some sort of perspective. For example, when a child whines it's annoying, but no one is hurt, so we could certainly ignore it and try to redirect her. A parent could say to a whining child, "I think you'd like to have your toy. I think you know how to ask for your toy in your big three-year-old way." Then, when the child asks correctly, the parent can express how good it feels to have him ask without whining.

Another effective technique when ignoring unwanted behavior is to wait for some time to pass without the behavior occurring, then catch children being good. When this happens, say something like, "What a wonderful vacation day we've had; there hasn't been any fighting at all. Thanks for making things so pleasant."

With positive reinforcement, good modeling from parents, and clear messages, children usually respond well to changes in their unwanted behaviors. They know that parents care enough to be patient and consistent, and that they will give them credit for each improvement made.

PARENTING POINTERS

➤ Before pushing for a change, parents should assess a child's developmental level to determine if modifying a behavior is realistic.

➤ Kids respond best to clear direction and positive reinforcement when changing a behavior.

➤ One of the most effective ways parents can influence a child's behavior is to set a good example through their own actions.

➤ Parents should make an effort to catch their children being good and express pride in their behavior.

41. Sibling rivalry
Helping kids get along

Helping brothers and sisters get along is one of the greatest concerns of parents with more than one child. Constant battles over toys, games and parental attention can be exhausting for the entire family. While competition and arguing among siblings is normal, there are steps that parents can take to help diffuse the tension.

Parents can start by modeling cooperative behavior. Parents should express feelings, argue, and resolve conflicts with each other in ways that children can model. If children can see parents calmly discussing differences and reaching a compromise, they may be able to adapt the same strategy.

Whenever possible, parents should try to stay out of children's arguments. When a child comes to report, "He started it first," the parent need not respond automatically. Consider who kept the fight going and think about the real reason behind the disagreement. Also, parents should review their own anxiety when children fight. Just because a parent is anxious about his children fighting doesn't mean that he needs to stop the fight. Determine when the fight must be stopped, such as when a child is in danger of being hurt physically.

Notice if fighting is happening at particular times, such as when kids are hungry, bored, tired, or just plain tired of being with each other. Then, try to anticipate these situations and avoid them. Making sure lunch is on time or limiting time spent on a tiring activity can go a long way toward avoiding bickering.

It's important to allow both competition and cooperation to occur between children in a family. Children learn to use social skills and how to get along in the world by interacting with their siblings. However, parents should give each child individual attention. Tune into the child's needs and appreciate her as an individual. By building up each child's self-esteem, the rivalry among siblings may lessen.

Some parents are concerned about their children's relationship because they want the children to be close friends when they grow up. However, fighting in childhood does not predict distant or hostile sibling relationships in adulthood. It is important to remember that conflicts occur in some way in all families. Parents may be able to moderate them at times, but it is normal for conflicts to occur.

In the family setting children learn how to live, love, laugh, fight and cry with others. As a result, kids learn to cope with conflict and to resolve it throughout their lives. While many parents still feel uncomfortable when children don't get along, it is not always a problem that needs to be fixed. It may be that at times the problem is the parent's discomfort rather than the kids' fights.

PARENTING POINTERS

➤ Children can learn important skills through conflict with their siblings. Parents can help by teaching mediation skills.

➤ Parents shouldn't automatically intervene in every sibling fight.

➤ Parents need to think about their own anxiety and consider whether that is what is motivating them to break up a fight.

➤ Fighting and squabbling in childhood does not mean that siblings won't get along later in life.

42. Anger
Helping children adapt, confront and escape

For many children (and adults) anger is one of the most common unpleasant feelings. It is also one of the most difficult to manage properly. When anger is mishandled it can disrupt families and strain relationships at home. Teaching a child to use anger constructively is a crucial job for parents who want to create a home environment that fosters emotional growth.

Parents can teach their children that there are three fundamental responses to anger. First, they can adapt to the situation. Second, they can confront the source of the stress, or third, they can escape from the situation.

Children should understand that the first and most important use of anger is for self-change. When a child adapts to anger he is changing what he's doing in response to the situation. When a child becomes frustrated or angry, he may suddenly have a great deal of energy. The amount of anger may depend on how he interprets the situation. However, the frustration can be channeled in a positive way. For example, a child might become angry at a math teacher for assigning a certain set of problems. He might be frustrated and angry because he isn't doing as well in math as he'd like. Rather than become angry, a child can be shown how to channel his feelings by studying harder, taking more notes, or asking the teacher to explain how to do certain problem he doesn't understand. Often this approach will solve things, and the anger will disappear.

The next option is to confront the source of stress or anger. First
the child should identify what is causing the hurt, then confront the
other person to correct the situation. Children are often successful
using this method in a tactful way. They can be taught to stay calm
and tell the person what they want, listen to the response, and pro-
pose a compromise agreement. For example, when a child is bothered by a little brother when she's trying to do her homework, the
natural tendency is to get angry. Instead of lashing out, she can confront him by saying: "Please stop asking me to play with you; leave
me alone for the next half hour so I can get my homework done. After
that I'll play with you. Meanwhile, why don't you set up the game for
us to play when I finish?"

The third option to cope with anger is to escape from the stressful
situation. This is easier for adults than children, since children and
adolescents don't usually have many feasible "escape" options from
frustrating situations. But when a child has tried to adapt to a frustrating situation and then attempted to ask the other person to change
with no success, he can decide not to associate with that person any
more, or at least for quite a while. He might need to stop trying to do
something that keeps frustrating him. For example, he might quit a
soccer team if he keeps getting upset during practice or games. However, adapting or confronting an angry situation, rather than escaping, usually works best for a child and it builds confidence and social
skills. So, if a child thinks he needs to escape, he should ask an adult,
such as a parent, about his decision before he takes action.

PARENTING POINTERS

➤ Parents should encourage children to channel their anger into
positive ways by changing their own behavior and adapting to frustrating situations.

➤ Children can be very effective at managing anger by confronting the source of their stress and negotiating a resolution.

➤ When children are in frustrating situations in which adapting
or confronting the anger doesn't work, escaping the situation — at
least for a while — may be appropriate.

43. Effective commands
Providing direction that gets results

Getting kids to listen and respond is never easy. It takes time and patience to help kids develop self-control and learn to cooperate. Parents and kids alike respond differently depending on how a message is delivered. Sometimes just changing the manner in which parents give commands to their children can solve or avert the problem. Following are a few pointers that can help parents be more effective in getting children to follow directions.

First, parents need to mean and enforce what they say. It does no good to make a request that a parent doesn't expect to be followed to its completion. When a child is asked to do something — whether it's organizing her room or turning off the television — it's important to back it up. A child is not going to learn if she is instructed to pick up her room, only to have her parent do it in the end. Be ready to respond with appropriate consequences, either positive or negative, to show that you mean what you have said.

Commands need to be stated simply and directly. It doesn't help to present the command as a question or a favor. For example, "Would you mind setting the table for me?" is not very effective. That approach gives the child an "out." If a child doesn't hear your request, she can't act on it. A parent can start by looking at the child and getting eye contact. If necessary, gently turn her face toward yours to ensure that she's listening and watching. A common mistake is for a parent to try to give instructions while a child is watching television or engaged in another activity. With something so much more entertaining going on, a parent's instructions can't compete. Ask the child to turn from these distractions before speaking to her.

Parents also need to limit the number of commands given together. Most children are only able to follow one or two instructions at a time. If a task is complicated, consider breaking it down into smaller steps. Asking a child to first gather dirty clothes into a pile, and then telling her to take them downstairs may work.

Another good technique is for the parent to ask the child to repeat the request. This doesn't have to be done each time, but it can help when the parent isn't sure she has been heard or understood. Repeating commands also helps with children who have short attention spans.

When a child is old enough to have jobs around the home it can be useful to make up chore cards for each job. This can be a three-by-five card with the steps involved in the chore clearly written. Then, when a child is supposed to do that chore, the parent hands her the card and says that this is what needs to be done. This can reduce the amount of arguing over whether she has done the chore properly. Another option would be to indicate on the card how much time the chore should take. Set the kitchen timer for that amount to help her know exactly when it should be done.

PARENTING POINTERS
➤ Parents should show a child how to do a job and let him try it.
➤ Parents should be ready to back up requests with positive or negative consequences.
➤ Provide feedback. Let the child try a task again.
➤ When a child does a good job, reward her success.

44. Cooperation
Tools to help children learn to be responsible

Every parent's fantasy is a peaceful home where a child cheerfully responds to requests to clean up her room or share a toy with a sibling. But that's not reality. At times, depending on the child's age, he may be very eager to cooperate. At other times, he may be obstinate. Parents need to remember what expectations are appropriate at what age. Keeping that in mind, there are many opportunities at home to teach kids how to cooperate.

Children can handle different tasks at different ages. For example, young children can be expected to help take care of themselves by washing their hands or dressing themselves. School-age children can move on to more complex chores, such as setting the table or dusting the furniture. A teen can be expected to do her own laundry or to help make dinner, even if her choice for dinner or timing of the laundry differs from her parents.

Parents should try to respect the way a child completes a task; this can encourage cooperation. It is no fun to try something new only to be criticized by a parent. When children help out at home, not only does it help the household run smoothly, it can give the children a sense of pride. It builds confidence, respect for others, and responsibility.

Pitching in with chores helps kids feel part of a team. Getting the whole family to work together on a fun project can foster a sense of teamwork. This could be building a tree house, planning a vacation, or organizing a birthday party. These joint efforts build trust and

togetherness. If the group task is interesting enough, it may even
motivate children to perform less appealing chores.

Even when something unexpected occurs during a cooperative project, kids can learn. For example, if a six-year-old carries in a cake only to have it flip and land face down, everyone can work together to frost it again. Working as a team has the added benefit of helping children who are struggling with sibling rivalries to discover that each child is important and can make their own unique contribution.

What happens when a child says no to a cooperative venture? Then a parent must decide whether to force the issue, based on whether the requested behavior is essential. If so, a system of consequences will need to be enacted. On the other hand, it may just be a matter of timing and success may come with a repeat approach on another occasion.

In cooperative families each member plays a vital role in maintaining the home. Knowing that they make a contribution can help children feel secure and valued in the family. Although they may not appreciate it at the time, children are learning habits that they'll perform for the rest of their lives.

PARENTING POINTERS

➤ Children will be more cooperative when given choices. For example, when appropriate, give a child a choice of chores.

➤ Parents should recognize when a child does the job well and commend her on any new skills learned. On the other hand, if jobs aren't done follow through with consequences.

➤ Understand that kids are not going to be perfect. There will be times when a child needs to be creative, be messy, go barefoot, or have their own space.

➤ Provide activities for the family to work on together, projects that can teach cooperation as well as be fun.

45. Television
Understanding its impact and establishing limits

Most parents are concerned about the amount of time their children spend watching television, and rightfully so. The consensus among experts today is that excessive TV viewing can be detrimental to children. But parents can control the influence of television by screening programs, limiting viewing time, and watching programs with kids.

Before deciding how to regulate the TV at home, parents should first understand why it is important to do so. One very practical reason is that the child who spends many hours watching may not be learning to relate to his peers. Forming friendships with other kids is an important developmental task for all children. If this isn't accomplished growing up, then adult social skills can be much harder to master.

Secondly, too much TV can lead to a passive orientation about life. Kids who spend hours in front of the television may not be developing the mastery of their bodies and minds. They're not being active or productive either. As a result, they miss out on the satisfaction that comes from accomplishing something, such as learning to play a new game, riding a bike, or building a model of something. These achievements help to make a child feel good about himself and develop self-confidence to take on new challenges.

The most pressing problem about too much TV is the effect of violence and sexual stimulation on children. Some children can deal with the more frightening aspects of TV shows, while others clearly can't. The results range from serious fears to sleep disturbances. Much of the impact of TV is a result of how the individual child processes what he sees. So, if a child seems bothered by sleep disturbances or significant fears, a parent might need to take into account the effect TV may be having on her.

One way that parents can offset this potential negative effect of TV is to view the programming with their children. This allows the parent to monitor the content of programs and to be available for comments and explanations or to change the channel. Parents also can help kids separate fact from fiction by explaining that scenes portrayed on the screen are not real.

Television viewing certainly isn't all bad. There are many informative and enriching programs, particularly on public television. Parents, however, should select programs for their children carefully and restrict the total amount of TV watched by their children. A good recommendation is that children watch no more than one hour of TV per night. Younger children at home may watch several short programs or a video during the day, interspersed with active play.

And what about homework... should it be completed before children watch television? As a rule, we should work before we play. If a half hour of TV before homework is relaxing, then sometimes it helps to permit this limited amount of recreation first.

Sometimes parents use TV as a reward or a punishment. If chores or homework are completed, then allowing children to watch TV can be a good reward. On the other hand, if grades in school are slipping, TV watching can be limited.

The most important consideration for parents about their children's TV viewing is that parents need to be aware that children respond to programs very differently than adults. For that reason, it's imperative that parents both monitor programs and restrict the amount of hours their children spend in front of the TV to guard against any negative effects. Collaborating with parents of a child's friend about limiting TV viewing during visits can be helpful too.

PARENTING POINTERS

➤ Since excessive TV viewing can hurt kids by creating passivity and low attention skills, parents should intervene with viewing rules.

➤ When parents watch TV with kids they can help explain what's happening and answer questions.

➤ Parents should screen programs and limit time kids spend watching TV, otherwise children have less time to build social and reading skills.

46. Bullies
Helping kids stand up for themselves

When a child is frightened of a bully who has been bothering him, parents find themselves in a tough situation. The child doesn't want to appear to be a "baby" by having the parent stand up for him, yet the child may need some coaching or parental intervention.

If the bully is using threats or physical intimidation, the parent should encourage his child to try to handle the situation himself by using the strengths that he has, without resorting to physical violence. These strengths may be a sense of humor, verbal skills, or a strong sense of self that lets him walk away from the situation. For example, a good sense of humor, even in a ten-year-old, can sometimes really hit home to a big kid who is using only brawn against smaller kids. A bully only knows how to respond with more violence, so a child may find success with these different responses that throw the bully off guard.

Parents can help at home without embarrassing the child. One way is with role playing. Since it's important that the child doesn't look scared, a parent can teach the child to stand up taller and appear confident. Or, try some role reversal games, such as "You be the bully, and I'll be you." This game could help the child see things from the other's point of view and understand why the bigger kid acts the way he does. A basic technique for defusing a bully situation for children is to learn to ignore the bully, since bullies want to know that they upset the victim. Other techniques include predicting the situation and rehearsing a verbal response. Where possible, simply avoiding the person works too.

Although most parents want to teach their children not to hit or fight, there is a danger that the child will turn into a perennial victim. Encouraging a child not to hit doesn't mean that the child shouldn't know how to protect himself against aggressors. Helping the child to be more active and not so passive is one way to enhance his self-confidence in standing up to bullies. For example, when a child is being harassed on the way home from school, the child might predict where it will happen and choose another route or arrange to walk with a friend. He could also have a safety plan, including places to stop at a friend's or neighbor's home.

Parents can also try to help their child think of other ways to counteract a bully. For example, maybe the child's friends can help, since they are probably frightened too. The parent can act as a consultant to the child, and sometimes this may help alleviate the problem as the child finds his own solutions.

But the parent should watch for signs that the child is overly upset by the situation. Is he afraid to go to school? Is he having recurrent nightmares or wetting the bed? These may be signs that there is a serious problem. If this is the case, a parent can try to intervene either directly by calling the other child's parent or perhaps discreetly by calling a teacher or counselor. Someone in authority at the school may be able to help if made aware that there is a problem between the two children.

PARENTING POINTERS

➤ Parents can encourage a child to use his own strengths, such as humor, to fend off a bully.

➤ Role playing can empower a child and help him understand the perspective of a bully.

➤ While parents can discourage violence, a child also needs to know how to protect himself against aggressors.

➤ If a bully situation escalates, a parent should contact the other parent or someone at school to help mediate.

47. Nagging
How to avoid harping at your children

No one likes to be told over and over what to do. But it takes repetition for kids to learn how to do certain things, so parental "nagging" seems hard to avoid. Yet, most parents eventually realize that they waste a lot of time and energy haranguing their children.

If parents find themselves repeating commands without compliance, they probably need to find other ways to communicate with their child and to examine the tone of their message. The parent's tone may be sarcastic, angry, or condescending without him being aware. It helps for the parents to tone down their emotional reactions as they repeat requests to the child.

Sometimes parents are too wrapped up in their child's every action. Parents can benefit from having their own activities to keep busy, such as gardening or reading. Then, when tempted to nag or overreact to a situation with a child, a parent can direct energies to this other project instead. Focusing energy elsewhere and keeping the situation in perspective can really help.

A spouse or another family member also can help a parent who nags too much work to change the behavior. Other adults can act as a consultant with open-ended comments such as, "How do you think your approach with Jimmy is working?" It's better for the other parent to wait until the confrontation with the child has passed before discussing the techniques. At a more relaxed time, the other parent will be more effective in getting the nagging parent to take a more objective look at how he's handling the situation. Any question asked calmly is better received by the listener.

Often nagging or overreacting is the result of a parent spending too much time worrying about the child or other factors, such as stress. In these instances, the other parent can volunteer to take over the responsibility for awhile. "Would you mind if I tried a new approach with Joey? You take a break for a few weeks." Offer relief to a parent stuck in an ineffective pattern of continual nagging without results.

Parents stuck in nagging behavior may also have to develop a more positive attitude toward their child. Changing their focus to emphasizing good behaviors that inevitably occur from time to time, rather than focusing on repeated negative behavior, may help the parent-child relationship. Just a few affirmations and complements when deserved during the day will build a new pattern of positive communication. Slowly, the child will seek more approval and begin to comply in some other areas, which may lead to a positive cycle of improvement in the very areas that caused the initial nagging.

When nagging starts to dominate the parent's communication with a child, change needs to occur. Parents need to step back, re-evaluate their strategies, get feedback from other supportive adults, and find new ways to interact with their child.

PARENTING POINTERS

➤ Parents need to have their own activities and interests to keep them from being too controlling and negative toward their children.

➤ It can be useful for parents to discuss parenting strategies together. This way the nagging parent can receive some feedback and direction about how to be more effective.

➤ All children have good qualities that need to be nourished. Focusing on a child's positive behavior can fend off the temptation to criticize.

➤ Parents should make certain that they are not taking out stress and anger from their life on the kids.

48. Planning
Minimizing accidents and confrontations

Parents are most successful when they are attentive to the needs of their children and plan ahead. Creating a child-friendly environment at home and carefully planning activities can help kids thrive. Consider these three tactics to help avoid problems:

1. Can the child's environment be changed to make accidents or confrontations less likely?

2. Can the parent prepare the child for any changes in his environment to avoid an intense reaction on the child's part?

3. Can the parent and child plan future events together, so the child is well prepared?

A parent who uses these strategies is showing the child as much respect and consideration for his feelings as the parent would show a spouse or friends. Children aren't really any different than adults when it comes to doing something new or something that might bring disapproval from others. But try not to wait until a child makes a mistake; rather, help him avoid it. He will be far less defensive before a problem occurs than after the fact.

A child also appreciates it when a parent keeps him informed about future events, since kids like to know what's coming next to give them time to adjust. If friends are coming to visit, for example, a parent can explain to him what they will be doing together and what is expected of him, as well as which areas of the house will be off limits to him. This works much better than issuing negative commands to him when the company arrives. And the child will be happy to have the parent's acceptance and to know that the parent has confidence that he will be able to comply.

The best way to prevent accidents with young children is to thoroughly child-proof the home. Carefully inspect the house for problem areas where kids can get hurt or into trouble. Remove breakable or dangerous objects and keep medicines out of reach or locked. Make sure toys are in good condition, splinter-free, and contain no loose parts. Also consider using only unbreakable glasses and cups to avoid messes. Put up gates on stairways to protect young kids. Keep safety tips in mind, such as staying with small children during baths.

Another way to plan ahead is to change aspects of a child's environment to reduce conflict. Here are some examples for young children:

• Create a separate area in the home or garage for play.

• Buy clothes that are easily washable.

• Keep a stool handy so a child can reach to hang up his own clothes and get items he needs.

• Designate a separate area in the yard for digging, planting.

• Erect a fenced-in play area for youngest kids to be safe outside.

• Provide an easel for painting.

• Keep plastic place-mats to protect your tablecloth.

• Maintain a variety of toys that are handy in various areas of the house.

A child who sees his parent making such an effort to change his environment to make him safer and happier will feel loved and valued for his own needs and talents.

PARENTING POINTERS

➤ Parents should take the time to thoroughly child-proof the home to help kids avoid getting hurt or into trouble.

➤ Designing special play areas and child-friendly space can help a kid feel safe and loved.

➤ By communicating with children about future plans parents can help children be prepared and reduce possible conflict.

49. Homework
How much should parents be involved?

Homework can turn into a battleground between parents and children if there is not a clear understanding of rules and expectations. The purpose of homework is to reinforce and complement the learning acquired in school. This can be lost or undermined if homework becomes a conflict in the family. Parents can be successful by setting certain guidelines and talking with children about the responsibility of homework.

The degree to which parents should actually help with homework depends on a number of factors: the child's age and grade, the difficulty of the assignment, and the extent of the resources that the child has at his disposal. In some cases, it is appropriate to help with assignments; other times it's better just to explain the directions to the child, work together on one example, and then let the child complete the assignment alone. An older child who can refer to books in the family library needs far less help than a primary school child who is just beginning to master penmanship and number concepts. In any event, the parent should act as a consultant or guide and not do the work for the child.

The younger child who wants a parent to remain during the homework session may be experiencing feelings of separation and is more concerned with companionship than the assistance. If a parent chooses to honor the child's request, the child must understand that the responsibility for the homework is still his.

The parent's role is not to demand that the homework be done in a certain way. Instead, parents should be encouraging and provide an environment that will motivate the child in the homework process. Parents need to convey their value of education so that the child will understand the importance of the homework. For example, parents can establish a time reserved for homework with no play, telephone calls, or television. If this "homework window" is enforced consistently, children begin to understand that homework is an integral part of home life that their parents expect to be done. The parent can help the child identify what he doesn't know and figure out what to ask the teacher. A study area that is specially designated for homework facilitates the process, too.

The amount of time devoted to homework varies with age and grade. The rule of thumb is the lower the grade, the less time a child should need. Certainly, homework shouldn't consume the entire evening for any age child. If a child is spending an excessive number of hours doing homework, parents need to make certain that the child understands the concept. Perhaps their child is having some difficulty in school that needs to be addressed or perhaps the teacher is assigning too much work.

Other children in the family can also help younger children with their homework. This works well because it eliminates the natural power struggle that occurs between parents and children. When children help each other it's a mutual learning process. The child who doesn't know the material will learn at least a little, and the tutoring child will have his knowledge reinforced. Everybody wins in this situation.

The biggest homework dilemma faced by parents is what to do if the child doesn't do it. When a child refuses to do homework, it's the school's responsibility to respond with appropriate consequences. If parents have provided the basic structure, encouraged the child to do the assignments, and made themselves available for questions, they've lived up to their end of the bargain. However, by communicating frequently with teachers when problems arise, parents can increase the chance for success. The children will learn about the consequences of their actions if they receive a detention slip or poor grade. This is often enough to create change without parents administering additional punishment, such as grounding or taking away privileges.

If a teacher calls and complains that the child is not doing the assigned homework, the parent should inquire what the teacher plans to do about it. The teachers' responsibility is to stimulate the child and provide opportunities for learning — and, if necessary, to take appropriate measures if assignments aren't completed. The parent still bears the responsibility to support the teacher's efforts and to hold fast to home rules about time and place for homework. This may mean that TV or other privileges are not granted unless homework time is respected.

Basically, schools should teach and parents should parent, but each must support the other's efforts. Problems arise when one tries to fulfill the role of the other. A collaborative relationship should exist between home and school, so that parents and teachers can support each other in helping the child learn.

PARENTING POINTERS

➤ The amount of parental involvement in homework varies depending on the child's age, the assignment, and the resources available.

➤ Parents can help kids complete their homework by setting specific study times and providing a suitable learning environment at home.

➤ Children can often learn with the assistance of siblings or other family members.

➤ If children do not complete their homework, they should face the consequences at school and at home. It is their responsibility alone.

50. Generosity
Developing a willingness to help others

Children can become so wrapped up in their own world of toys, clothes, and friends that parents often worry whether they are raising selfish kids. It's natural, however, for children to be self-centered. As they grow up, kids must focus on their own needs as they become unique individuals. This self-absorption will decrease as children mature and they begin to consider the needs of others.

It's important for parents to understand that what would be selfishness in adults isn't necessarily selfish behavior in a child. The seemingly "selfish" behavior or attitude may simply be a reflection of the child's natural view of himself as the center of his world. Parents need to use different standards of judgment with children. For example, a child's demand to have a parent help him get a special object for show and tell the next day, despite the fact that it's his parent's busiest workday, does not mean he's selfish. He's simply focusing on his own world.

Despite a child's sometimes egocentric perspective on the world, there are positive things a parent can do to foster generosity and willingness to help others. Initially, parents should praise children when they demonstrate empathy or compassion in their children. The ability to put oneself in another's place is one of the foundations of generous behavior. Parents can feel reassured if they realize that their children have this basic capacity and value system.

Parents should be cautious about imposing adult standards of altruism on their child. Don't force unselfishness on kids. Altruism is far more likely to develop into a meaningful life value if it unfolds naturally. Parents should try to avoid saying things like, "If you were a nice boy, you'd shovel our elderly neighbor's walk." This might work temporarily, but it doesn't help cultivate ongoing empathy. That needs to come from within the child. Instead, a parent may point out that the elderly neighbor can't get out to shovel his walk — merely highlight the need — and see if the child takes the initiative to help. Or a parent and child can shovel the walk together and talk about the good feeling that results from helping others.

Example is the most powerful teacher. Kids live what they see, so if generosity is a family value and it's demonstrated frequently, it becomes easier for kids to make it a part of their lives. When kids see their parents participate in volunteer projects they have an example to emulate. If mom or dad collects for a charity or serves on a community project, this makes the point far more dramatically than a dozen talks about the issue.

Organizations such as churches, schools, and scouts offer excellent programs to encourage families and children to reach out to others. Parents can take advantage of these group opportunities that foster altruism and let kids have fun in the process. Maybe instead of a regular summer camp, a child or a family may opt to participate in a work trip with a church youth group or charitable group. The experience of helping flood victims rebuild or teaching disadvantaged children can leave a lasting impression about the value of service. Also, working side by side on a common cause can strengthen family ties and friendships.

Try to find ways to include the whole family in service projects, so children can learn first-hand the joy of giving. Together, a family might serve at a soup kitchen, build housing for the poor, or help a less fortunate family during the holidays. Children likely will remember these events for some time. If helping others is initially associated with a pleasant experience, it's more likely to be repeated and incorporated into the child's life.

PARENTING POINTERS

➤ While children's behavior may seem selfish at times, parents should remember that it is developmentally natural for children to focus on their own needs.

➤ Parents can encourage children to be giving, but should not force it.

➤ Parents can best motivate their children to develop a spirit of generosity by modeling volunteerism and service themselves.

➤ Participating in service projects as a family is a great way to teach children the joy of volunteering while having fun as a family.

51. Getting organized
How to help kids handle new routines

Growing up means learning to do more. Every year kids start new activities and take on more responsibilities at school and at home. Parents can help children meet these new challenges in a positive, organized, stress-free way.

Organization doesn't happen instantly. It takes a while for everyone to adjust to a new routine. Children eventually can learn to plan and follow a new schedule, with the help of a caring adult. But parents should be realistic and not expect too much too fast. And it helps not to be focused on perfection.

It's helpful to remind kids that, just as they learned to ride a bike step by step, they need to learn new routines and responsibilities one step at a time. These daily routines might include taking the bus, going to school, doing homework, and participating in sports or activities. Balancing all this can take practice and careful planning. Added responsibilities might include walking a dog, making a bed, or taking piano lessons.

Lines of communication need to stay open. Children should be encouraged to talk about how they are handling changes at school or new activities. One way to help children adjust to new routines is to set time aside for family meetings where everyone can discuss schedules, routines, and chores. Parents can be flexible, letting a child give up some established chore for a few weeks when he is getting used to a new routine or activity.

Talking with kids is important, but timing is critical. When kids return home from school, sometimes they need a few moments alone to unwind. Parents shouldn't bombard them immediately with questions. If a parent needs to talk about upcoming plans or activities, he could say, "Perhaps when you feel like talking about … When can we get together?" or "When can we talk about it?"

Be aware when a child is stressed or upset by a new routine or activity. Help him identify the feeling. Approach him by saying, "I see you're upset" or "Something must have happened in school today to make you so angry." Many times by expressing himself the child will solve his own problem without the parent offering advice or controlling the situation.

When given the support and help they need to organize their time and deal with any frustrations, children will eventually do well with new routines and activities. They need to know that someone understands their challenges and appreciates their hard work in taking on more grown-up responsibilities each year.

PARENTING POINTERS

➤ Parents need to be supportive and patient when kids take on new activities and responsibilities.

➤ Communication among family members can help everyone ease into new schedules.

➤ Parents should look for signs of stress in children as they learn to adapt to new situations.

Parents Are People Too

52. Parental stress
Tips for keeping perspective

Raising children is a stressful, round-the-clock job that often goes unappreciated. While the warmth of a child's hug goes a long way to keeping a parent going, stress is a natural byproduct of parenting. The constant demands of parenting mean that parents have little time left for themselves. This can leave parents feeling even more stressed and resentful.

Not only do adults have no formal training for the demanding role of parenting, but the job duties are always changing. There is no magical "parental instinct" that automatically equips people to care for children. Parents can feel overwhelmed if they think they should have all the answers. But there are ways to cope with this overload — through communication, activities, and planning — that can reduce stress for both parents and children.

Parents can start by examining their expectations. Mom and dad need to ask themselves honestly if they expect too much from their kids. For example, a five-year-old, however lovable, isn't very neat, usually doesn't listen the first time, and likes to fight with siblings. So, if parents are expecting behavior more suitable for a child who's a year or two older, they'll be disappointed. Setting unrealistic expectations can lead to stress.

Rather than let anger build up, parents need to find a supportive adult (preferably the same age and one who has children) to talk to about the issues causing their stress. Keeping feelings inside can lead to a more serious explosion later. Also, parents should ask friends and relatives for occasional help. Having someone else watch the children for a few hours can allow a needed break. The parent can return refreshed and less stressed.

Parents also need to communicate with their children. They should tell their kids what makes them angry. After all, adults have feelings too. If the situation is escalating and the parents are losing control, they need to leave the room for a minute. They will be able to deal with the kids more effectively when they are calm.

Planning for hectic times with kids reduces stress, too. For example, if bedtime is stressful, parents can set up a routine — snack, bath, stories, bed — so kids know what to expect. A predictable schedule of what to do each night can make the time less harried. Also, try to avoid unnecessary changes that can add to stress, such as a different room or new bed before the child is ready.

Another effective strategy is for parents to shift their focus from their children to themselves. Daily exercise — even walking up and down the stairs for 10-15 minutes — will help reduce stress. After the kids go to bed, read, talk about vacation plans, or watch a funny television show. It's amazing how therapeutic laughter can be.

PARENTING POINTERS

➤ Parents can reduce stress in their lives by letting their kids act their age and not setting unrealistic expectations for their behavior.

➤ Sharing stress with others and getting time away from children can help parents keep their emotions in check.

➤ Thinking ahead and avoiding too much change can lessen stress.

➤ Parents need to take time for simple activities, such as exercise and laughter, to have a good balance in life.

53. Couplehood to parenthood
Making a smooth transition

The transition from being a couple to becoming parents can be tough. It is complicated by the fact that people marry and have children later in life. As a result, they have had more time alone to explore, develop their relationship, and enjoy being individuals, which can make the shift to becoming a family and putting children's needs first even more challenging.

A couple's relationship is the building block for the family's relationship. This is why it's important for couples to learn to communicate and negotiate together effectively before becoming parents. Couples who develop good communication skills have set the stage for a successful family. They can then provide the relationship model that their children will learn to use in their own lives.

In a secure relationship each individual will feel safe, accepted, and loved. Couples learn to recognize their feelings, while taking the time to identify their partner's concerns. This healthy respect for each other in marriage can provide a solid basis for a new family.

Once the work of being a couple is successfully in progress, the couple is ready to make the transition to parenthood. Whenever parenthood arrives, it is certain to require adjustments in the marriage. Parenthood may mean postponing or ending a career. And it can bring a profound change in expectations and perceptions of spouses.

Parents have time to prepare and fantasize about their life ahead during the pregnancy. But when the baby arrives the sometimes shocking reality of parenting a newborn sets in. It helps for parents to talk in advance about how they see their roles as parents. They should state their parenting goals positively; "I want to spend a good deal of time with my youngster" or "I want to have time alone with my wife or husband," or "I want to teach them this or that." These statements identify goals that can be worked on after the baby is born.

A new baby may require a number of sacrifices. Financially, families may be reduced from two incomes to one. In an age when success is so often defined by monetary means, the couple's self-worth may suffer. A new baby may mean delaying purchases for the home, curtailing vacations or limiting entertainment. For some parents just baby-proofing the house can be a challenge that's unsettling. Despite these challenges, parents also experience an abundance of joy and wonder with the arrival of a baby and the formation of a new family.

Parents may also have to give up sleep, long showers, meals out, time with friends, and other leisure activities. Parenting can be isolating, and finding new friends in like circumstances can be difficult. Neighborhoods today don't lend themselves to easy access of making new friendships as in the past, and extended family may not live nearby to offer advice and assistance. All of these factors may contribute to the need at times for parent support groups to help parents create new definitions for good parenthood.

The good news for young parents, especially those who have children later in life, is that they are usually in touch with their own needs. With a good sense of self, mature parents are able to understand that in addition to caring for their children they need to nurture their own relationship. Many couples have established bonds of trust and intimacy that are maintained in parenthood, helping them to avoid becoming totally absorbed by their child.

To maintain a strong relationship, couples may go on dates alone or spend time together talking after the baby has gone to bed. Sometimes the bonds created with the arrival of a new child can strengthen a marriage. If couples take the time to develop their relationship, children can be allowed to be children, rather than the main connection between mom and dad. The children will then be freer, happier, more self-aware, and capable of building healthier lives for themselves.

Today's parents can have a better chance of success when they have used the years of being a couple to develop intimacy and communication skills that transfer to a strong family life.

PARENTING POINTERS

➤ Couples who work on developing good communication and negotiation skills will have a better chance of maintaining a healthy relationship as parents.

➤ Parents may find that teaming up with other parents and finding support groups will help in the transition to parenthood.

➤ Couples who find time to nurture their own marriage and don't become too child-oriented can see their relationship strengthen over time.

54. Humor
Lightening the load with laughter

Parenting should be enjoyed, not endured. A good dose of laughter can lighten the parenting load and make family life fun. With all the stress in life today, successful parents have discovered the benefit of using humor. Since life is 10 percent how you make it and 90 percent how you take it, it helps to work on your perception of the events in your daily life. Parents can relieve stress by just not taking little conflicts so seriously.

With appropriate humor parents can minimize some of the inevitable family conflicts and strengthen bonds with their kids. It just takes a simple reminder to lighten up a little. Try using a humorous motto for life, "You don't have to attend every argument you're invited to" or "Some days you get the elevator; some days you get the shaft." Even the most exasperating situations can be funny when parents keep perspective and maintain a sense of humor.

What is humor? It's a life perspective, an attitude about how seriously to take ourselves. By noticing the flip-side of situations parents can learn to be less serious about themselves and how perfect they are as parents. Laughing about how ludicrous a situation may be and being willing to make fun of yourself can reduce the stress of handling the many trials of parenting. Utilizing humor, parents can begin to see things in more than one way.

Humor abounds in family life, especially around children. In fact, many of the fondest family memories come from the "funny" times. Who can forget the times little ones enchant parents with their misconceptions while parents bite their lips to hide their chuckles? Laughing at mistakes can help parents see how silly it is to pursue perfection.

Humor also lowers children's resistance to certain tasks and increases cooperation. When young children are being obstinate, a funny comment serves as a distraction and may motivate them to get the job done. Older kids respond better to the humor of the written word. A lighthearted note reminding a teen to clean her room or have it closed by the health department gets the point across while avoiding face-to-face conflict.

The focus of humor in parenting is preventative. It is an excellent tool to keep minor conflicts from escalating. But using humor when a child is already upset will only make the problem worse. Instead, capture the power of positive humor and use it to prevent small concerns from growing into larger conflicts. For example, parents can tailor the humorous approach to how the child sees things. Using a "monster spray" to make the fears of a young child vanish may be the ticket to help make the bedtime ritual easier.

All children have certain qualities or actions that make parents smile, laugh, and just feel wonderful. All their good attributes can be the salvation for parents when looking for the lighter side of situations.

Humor establishes trust. It shows the parents as flexible, accepting, and honest. As a coping strategy, it gives parents plenty of time to reframe a tough situation. Parents who use humor model it for their children and are giving them a tool to help manage some of life's frustrations and stresses.

PARENTING POINTERS

➤ Humor can help reduce conflicts and bring a family closer together.

➤ Parents can focus on their children's joyful qualities to help get through stressful situations.

➤ Using humor can be a coping strategy for parents, giving them time to think through a difficult time.

55. Making amends
How parents can explain their mistakes

Most parents know they are not perfect as individuals or as parents. It is one thing for parents to manage their own shortcomings, but it's more difficult to explain these to children. Often, children have felt the pain of the parent's mistake. This may be a be a missed opportunity to give praise, a spanking, or a time when a parent was too absorbed in other problems to listen to a child. Fortunately, there are ways to reflect on these mistakes and make amends.

Making amends does not mean that a parent must wash away the deeds as though they never happened. It does mean that the parent should do what she can to "wash the wound clean," whether it's a minor incident or a major hurt, so the healing can begin.

The hurt that a child feels when he is confused about a parent's behavior can affect his self-esteem. The behavior may lead a child to conclude "I'm bad," "I'm stupid," or "There's something wrong with me." When a parent tries to make amends and hold a light to her own mistakes, a child can clearly see he is not being blamed or at fault. A child sees a parent who, while imperfect, still takes time to make peace with her own mistakes. This can teach the child fairness in parent-child conflicts.

The first step toward making amends is for the parent to take ownership and responsibility for what happened. This is more than an apology. Even if a child's behavior was out-of-bounds, the parent needs to examine what feelings were stirred up. For example, was the parent afraid of losing control, looking bad, or feeling foolish in some way? And did this influence the response?

Next, let the child off the hook. The parent should tell the child what feelings led to the action. The parent should assure the child that the parent is responsible for his own behavior and the child did not create the response. If the child's behavior was inappropriate, the parent can acknowledge that as a separate issue to confront.

It is important during this discussion to acknowledge the child's feelings. The child may feel let down, sad and mad. The parent can help identify the child's feelings and assure the child that he wants to hear about these feelings. Although the parent is admitting his shortcomings, he needs to stay in charge as a parent. Acknowledging mistakes does not mean that the parent has lost authority in dealing with his children. The parents still determine the rules of the home.

While this process may be difficult, parents need to recognize their own efforts and allow themselves to feel some satisfaction in having opened up to their children. Parents can silently begin and end every atonement made to their child with an acknowledgment of their own worth and abilities.

PARENTING POINTERS

➤ Sometimes a child feels that when a parent makes a mistake that it was the child's fault. When making amends parents should be clear to the child that he was not at fault.

➤ Encourage a child to express her feelings of disappointment or hurt.

➤ Parents should explain why they are angry to assure the child that they didn't cause those feelings.

➤ Through the process of making amends, parents should maintain their authority and confidence in parenting.

56. A child's education
Defining the parental role

Parents want their children to succeed in school, but often are unsure about how involved they should be in their children's education. Children who do well in school often have close parental support. Yet many parents struggle to define their role and what they should expect from their children and the school.

First, parents have an obligation to prepare children for school. This means sending children into the classroom who are rested, well fed, and not preoccupied with stress. At home, parents should establish a time and place for learning. A quiet area should be set up with good lighting and adequate materials for studying. Also, parents should help children develop behaviors, such as good manners and respect for others, that can foster learning in a group.

In order to reinforce what teachers are doing in the classroom, parents can highlight learning in everyday activities. For example, while cooking dinner a parent can discuss measurement. Laundry can be linked to the ideas of sorting and categorizing. While watching TV, plots can be discussed and children can guess as to what will happen next.

In addition to promoting learning at home parents need to monitor what is happening in school. Parents can do this by asking their children open-ended questions, such as "What was the most interesting thing you did in class today?" Through these discussions children will learn that their parents value education and are interested in their progress. It's also important for parents to become familiar with their child's work and materials. It is best to focus on the positives during these discussions. For example, a parent could point out the number of math problems the child got right on a paper before discussing difficulties.

Parents can support their children by getting involved in school activities and maintaining close communication with teachers. They can do this by attending PTA meetings and parent nights, introducing themselves to the principal, or by volunteering in the classroom. Teachers need to be aware of what is going on at home; parents need to be aware of what the school is trying to do. Parents can simply write a note, make a phone call, or arrange a meeting with a teacher to share information.

When having a teacher conference, parents should be prepared and take notes. (It's better if there are no children present at the conference; this can be awkward and stressful for the children.) It's a good idea to get specific instructions for helping children at home, that is, a prescription of sorts from the teacher. For example, the teacher might suggest, "Spell each vocabulary word five times and use it in a sentence," or "Use flash cards for ten minutes each night."

Parents basically delegate their responsibility to educate their child to the school, but they still play an important role, offering support to their child, providing a good study environment, and communicating with their child's educators. But it's important to remember that the child needs to "own" his work. The child is responsible for doing his own work. For example, when a child has written an essay for school, a parent can reinforce the notion of ownership by suggesting that the child read it aloud. The parent can then ask the child what she thinks about it and what areas she might wish to improve before offering any of his own comments.

If a teacher calls home with a problem the parents need not feel that they should have controlled the child's behavior at school. Instead, they need to work as a partner with the teacher in acknowledging the child's behavior and supporting the teacher's plan to improve the behavior with reinforcement at home.

When the child perceives a conflict with the teacher, it's best for the parent to help the child first brainstorm about possible solutions, and then confront the teacher himself if necessary. If the child is unsuccessful in working out the problem, the parent may need to get involved. He can remain friendly and keep an open mind in any discussion, first finding out the facts and feeling out the situation from the teacher, then talking about solutions. If the issues aren't resolved, the parent can then talk to the principal. The key point is that parents and teachers are a team; they reinforce each other and bring unique insights about the child to any learning solution.

PARENTING POINTERS

➤ Parents should provide a learning environment at home.

➤ By showing interest in children's school work, parents can monitor their development and convey the importance of education.

➤ Parents can support their children's education by getting involved in school activities and communicating frequently with teachers.

➤ It helps for parents to remember that children need to "own" their work. Likewise, children can be encouraged to find solutions on their own to problems at school. If needed, parents can then be of help.

57. Playing independently
Teaching kids to entertain themselves

Sometimes all a parent wants to do is talk on the telephone for a minute or cook dinner in peace, but children have a way of interrupting and demanding attention. The interruptions may seem constant and be more frequent just as the parent gets involved with a project. This can draw out even the simplest tasks and be frustrating. There are ways parents can teach their child to play independently when they need to be busy with some other activity.

First, parents should notice the child's efforts to please and praise the child for staying away and not interrupting. Most parents provide lots of attention to a child who's interrupting, but almost no attention to a child when he or she stays away, plays independently, and does not interrupt. No wonder kids interrupt parents so much — they get more attention that way.

When a parent is busy with some activity, like a phone call or work, she needs to give the child a direct command. This command should contain two instructions. One part will tell the child what to do while the parent is busy, and the second part will specifically tell him not to interrupt. For instance, say, "Mom has to talk on the telephone, so I want you to stay in this room and color and don't bother me. I'll come to see you when I'm finished."

Then, as the parent begins the activity, she should stop what she's doing for a moment, go to the child, and praise the child for staying away and not interrupting. Remind the child to stay with the assigned task and not to interrupt. Then wait a few more minutes before returning and again praising the child for playing alone. Return to the activity, wait a little longer, and again praise the child.

Over time, the parent can gradually reduce how often she praises the child, while increasing the length of time staying at her own task. If the child is about to leave what he was doing and come to interrupt, the parent should immediately stop what she's doing, go to the child and help redirect him to stay on task. The child's task should be something interesting like playing with a toy, watching TV, or coloring pictures.

Eventually, the parent will be able to stay busy for longer and longer time periods. As soon as the parent is finished, she should make sure to go to the child and provide special praise for letting her complete the task. Occasionally, the parent can give the child a small privilege or reward for having left her alone while working on a project.

Any activity can be enjoyed without constant interruptions if parents work on helping a child spend a few minutes alone. If a parent is trying to increase her ability to talk on the phone, for example, have a spouse or a friend call each day for awhile until the child adjusts. That way, when important calls come in, the parent and child will be ready to handle it.

PARENTING POINTERS

➤ Sometimes parents only give attention when a child is disruptive. A parent should give attention and praise when a child plays quietly and does not interrupt.

➤ Parents should give direct commands to children when they do not want to be bothered and offer the children alternative activities.

➤ As children learn to entertain themselves parents can offer praise and acknowledge their good behavior after short periods and eventually for longer periods.

58. Single parents
Overcoming challenges
to create a positive family life

Single parents know the challenge of parenting alone. There are numerous limits and constraints on a single parent, because there is no one else to share parenting tasks. Time, energy, and money often are limited, yet the same standards of parenting are applied to single parents as to everyone else, regardless of these limited resources. If a single parent takes on the parenting task with confidence and develops a reliable support system, children in single-parent households thrive.

It is helpful first to understand the challenges that a single parent faces. With only one adult in the home, there is essentially no buffer between the single parent and his or her children. Without a partner to serve as a sounding board or consultant, it can be difficult for a parent to maintain balance and objectivity. On the practical side, a single parent has to juggle several commitments between work, school meetings, and children's activities. This can leave a single parent feeling overwhelmed and stressed.

Pressures from society also take a toll on single parents. Single-parent families often are seen as different from the norm. These parents — 90 percent of whom are female — find that others may question their decision to parent alone. The single parent and the children often find themselves explaining the family situation to others. Children pick up on the idea that their family is somehow different. Labels, such as "broken home" also tend to devalue the family.

These stresses can leave a parent feeling isolated. Often the only

social network available is a homogenous group of other single parents, which helps to share resources, but doesn't provide access to the
larger community. As a result, single parents may not pursue social
and recreational activities, which can shortchange the whole family.
Studies have shown that children of single parents are affected in other
ways too. They are at a higher risk to become pregnant as teens, abuse
drugs, or display acting-out behavior.

Still, there are things single parents can do to make their situation
highly successful. Single parents who are divorced can promote a
healthy relationship with the parent not living in the home. By not
talking negatively about their absent partner or including children
in any conflicts, single parents can safeguard their children's belief in
both of their parents as positive parts of their lives. Preparing kids
for visits can also be part of the process of strengthening children's
belief that their family cares for them and is always available to support them.

Single-parent households can and do work successfully. When a
mother or father has good coping skills, a sense of control over her
life, and a strong community support system children can thrive.
When a parent can develop her "self" and gain a sense of competence, she conveys that confidence to the child. Then the child will be
able to say, "I'm resourceful, I'm clever, I know how to love and to
accept love." The child learns that his family can work out their own
system of love and support, and that he can count on its validation.

This positive self-image of a family is the most critical factor for
success. The family develops an internal closeness and a sense of confidence that things will work out, despite changes and fluctuations.
The key is that the family feels it can create its own success.

Indeed, single parents can turn disasters into opportunities when
they engage their children in dealing with feelings together as a unit.
Using simple language to communicate feelings like "mad," "sad," or
"scared," parents model problem solving and self-healing. Owning
the pain and talking about it, without denying its impact, helps kids
discover that they are also resourceful and durable. For example, helping a child express how sad he feels when he sees other families at a
restaurant with both parents and their children, can begin discussions of how his family offers special rewards too.

PARENTING POINTERS

➤ Single-parent families face a multitude of challenges with the pressures of limited time, resources, and often societal support.

➤ Successful single-parent households develop a sense of confidence that helps the family members maintain close ties.

➤ Tapping into the larger community and developing a network of friends can help single-parent families find needed support.

59. Fathering
The responsibilities and opportunities for dads today

Today fathers have new opportunities to get more involved in raising and forming close bonds with their children. Many want to interact more with their children, and businesses and the community are supporting the importance of the father's role in parenting. Traditionally, women have been the primary caregivers and nurturers. But as more women take jobs outside the home, the job of parenting is becoming more evenly divided. Children are the beneficiaries. They need the connection and influence of both their mother and their father as they grow up.

In families where the father is not involved, sometimes a child may misbehave to get the dad's attention. The child may even believe that by acting out he is demonstrating a need for a father's presence and extending an invitation for him to step in. Boys may act out with aggressive and disruptive behaviors, while girls may internalize their feelings, experiencing depression, anxiety, or sleep problems. Yet, even when it is clear to a father that he needs to be more involved with his children, he may not know how to do so, since his own father may not have been such a role model.

The father's traditional role of giving families a sense of security and control is still important. But many dads realize they must contribute more by getting more involved in the lives of their kids. Men looking to form closer relationships with their children can ask their wives for direction. Often, women have good communication skills and are in tune with how to relate to the children. Fathers can learn by observing these skills in action. Men should regard parenting as a team effort. Dads can get closer to their kids by participating in the routine tasks of doing homework, making dinner, and attending school activities.

Fathers need to be available to their children and to share a whole range of experiences with them. A child needs to know that her father is willing and able to make her a priority. For example, if a child comes home from school and is upset, she needs to feel her parent's interests and concerns. Children don't need constant attention. They do need the security of knowing that there is a reservoir of parental involvement to tap into when needed.

Regularly scheduled recreational activities also enhance relationships with children. Athletics have the combined advantage of offering structure and control, while promoting personal contact and interaction. Nevertheless, if the father and child's talents and interests lie elsewhere, they can find another activity to enjoy. Whether it's playing chess or shooting baskets together, fathers can connect with their children through shared activities.

When playing with children, fathers should try to just enjoy the interaction rather than setting goals for achievement. The point is companionship, not productivity. If a father overly invests in the game with performance expectations, he will defeat the purpose and may damage his child's self-esteem if that child cannot live up to the expectations.

Fathers and mothers are the most important role models for their children. That doesn't mean dads have to be perfect — or try to convince their children that they are. Fathers should deal with their own shortcomings with openness and honesty. Being a positive role model also means recognizing that one is not an unimpeachable authority. Fathers may have trouble admitting when they are wrong because they don't want to lose their children's respect. But, in truth, while it is valuable for children to see their father succeed, it can be more valuable for children to see their father successfully deal with failure.

Men are becoming more involved in their children's lives as fathers divide parenting responsibilities with their working wives and learn ways to better relate to their kids. Relationships with children are never static. There are always opportunities for growth and change.

The responsibility belongs to both the father and the child to com- municate and spend time together to build a positive relationship.

PARENTING POINTERS

➤ Fathers can form closer relationships with their children by being involved in their children's daily routines and activities.

➤ Setting up special times for just dads and kids to be together to play sports or cards can foster more intimate ties.

➤ Dads can be positive role models for their children by being honest about their strengths and weaknesses.

60. A parent's illness
Helping children cope and understand

When a parent is sick the whole family is affected. If mom or dad contracts a chronic, debilitating, or even terminal illness, the family's relationships and patterns inevitably are disrupted. Although the focus is on the sick parent, it is important for parents to take time to talk with and listen to the needs of the children in the family.

Children in such an uncertain situation have many fears. They need to know that they did not cause their parent's illness, that even when they are "bad" they could never do anything that would make mom or dad that sick. Kids may be concerned about not only what will happen to the parent, but what will happen to them. They often imagine terrible things — that they will be sent to an orphanage, or that they will get sick too. Parents should explain the situation and reassure the children.

When the parent's prognosis is unknown, and there is the possibility of a more serious illness or even death, children need to be prepared. There is no need to frighten them, however, if death is not imminent. Parents should talk about their feelings and encourage their kids to open up and voice their concerns. Children need to hear that the healthy parent or some caring relative can still keep the family together. "We'll all help out and we'll still live together as a family, no matter what happens" is the sort of message children need to hear.

Children should have as much information as possible about the illness, without frightening them. Instead of telling a young child, "In another year or so mom won't be able to walk," the parent can stress that "mom could get sicker...and she may not get better for a long time, or forever." But parents should respond honestly to questions from children rather than avoiding the truth. For instance, parents should explain to children how different medications may affect the sick parent. Some medications may make the parent sleepy; others cause changes in physical appearance, such as steroid drugs which make the face puffy, or other drugs which cause changes in skin coloring.

Dealing with adolescents during this time can be a challenge. They often tend to be centered on their own problems and resent the restrictions put on them when a parent is ill. Maybe the teens can't invite their friends over all the time or there is less money for the family to spend. Parents need to take the initiative to talk with teenagers. They can try to reflect the child's feelings with statements such as "It makes you angry that ..." and "I can't change anything, but you need to understand that ...." Families focused on an illness should approach problems creatively and learn to compromise. For example, maybe a parent can rest and have the TV brought into another room when the kids are having friends over.

When a parent is ill, everyone in the family must help out more with chores and other duties. Kids are almost always willing to help out, if approached in the right way. Some children want to know what is expected of them ahead of time; others can respond more immediately. By respecting these differences, parents can find ways for the work to get done. The important thing is that the family communicate and work together.

However, parents should guard against placing too much responsibility on children. When there are older children in the family, often the responsibility for the care of the younger children falls on their shoulders. Helping take care of the little kids is one thing, but the role of the parent is too much for them to handle.

Parents who are ill have to devote so much time to their illness — taking care of themselves, resting, taking medicines — that they may spend the rest of the time doing housework or catching up on practical things. But the parent needs to spend some of her good hours with the children. The healthy parent must also keep in mind the needs in the family and find time to spend time together.

When a family is faced with the death of a parent they may go through a number of stages including denial, anger, grief, and acceptance. How the parents handle these stages determines how the children will handle them too. The children need to know what is going on. The important thing is that children understand their parents' strengths and limitations more fully, while parents work to respect their children's feelings and needs as well.

PARENTING POINTERS

➤ Children of sick parents often have a range of fears, and parents need to reassure them that they will be cared for and loved.

➤ As much as possible, parents should explain the illness and medications to the children.

➤ Although both the sick and the healthy parent are pressed for time because of the disruptions to the family routine, parents need to make time to be with their children.

➤ Family members often are expected to take on additional tasks when a parent is ill, but parents should be careful not to pass along their parental responsibilities to older children.

61. Divorce
Coping with the impact on children

The termination of a marriage means much more than the end of a spousal relationship. With the marital separation comes the loss of dreams and a way of life. Understanding how children and adults are affected can help families cope with this major change.

During divorce adults often enter into a mourning process. They experience the same stages of mourning that generally accompany death of a loved one — shock, denial, depression, and anger. Even if the divorce comes as a relief, it can be followed by a long period of self-examination as the person struggles to regroup emotionally and rebuild a "single" lifestyle. Parents may feel guilty about divorce and, therefore, are tempted to be more lenient or generous with their children. However, in the midst of so much upheaval in their lives, children need routine, discipline and love as much as ever.

Children of divorce experience a whole range of emotions too. Their family, as they have known it, is no longer there. Children must accept their parents living in different places. Most tend to deny the situation at first. As the reality sets in they may begin to feel intense sadness, anger, and frustration because they can't make their world be the way they want it to be. They often feel confused about what the divorce means to them and become concerned about losing the other parent.

Many children of divorce wonder if they are to blame. Children often feel responsible and conclude that if they had behaved better the divorce wouldn't have happened. They may worry about practical issues, such as who will fix breakfast or sign their report card. There's also the fear that they will have to choose between parents. Children wonder if it will be safe to continue to show their affection and love for each of their parents.

Children naturally want all the significant people in their lives to get along. When that doesn't happen, young children in particular may feel insecure and frightened. Children's reactions to the divorce are often reflected in their behavior. The younger the child, the more regressive the behavior may seem. They may lose their most recently acquired skill, for example, dressing themselves or toilet training. A child who is anxious about the divorce simply doesn't have the energy to maintain these newly acquired behaviors.

Other behavior changes may include difficulties with aggression, not sharing, or whining. School-related concerns often surface, such as attention problems or an inability to get along with teachers or classmates. Under the stress of divorce, the child simply may not be able to keep up with everything and he may need to retreat and regroup. In addition, physical complaints such as headaches or stomach aches often indicate stress even before a child can verbalize his feelings.

Parents can help their children get through the divorce and reduce the stress by talking about what's going on in the family. They need to clarify that it's mom and dad who aren't getting along with each other, and that the children didn't cause the problem. And they can reassure the children that they will still be their parents. It's vital that children understand that they are not to blame and that they can't undo the situation.

Children may not have the words to describe how they feel about something painful, so parents need to initiate these conversations. Children should feel comfortable sharing feelings, concerns and fears. Of course, helping the children deal with their feelings places enormous demands on already stressed parents, but it's critical to the child's eventual adjustment. It's also important to support children in their relationship with the other parent. Parents should guard against letting their own negative feelings undermine the child's affection for the other parent. Parents can also do practical things, such as showing the child where the other parent will be living and explaining what will change and what will remain the same. They can also advise appropriate school personnel about the situation.

It's important to understand that it takes a long time to regain perspective after a divorce. Initially, both the parent's and the children's contacts with the ex-spouse may be overlaid with sadness, anger, or blame. Eventually, acceptance and forgiveness begin to replace those feelings and a renewed sense of competence for the entire family will emerge. The whole healing process can take from two to four years. It takes time, work, and a willingness to let go to adjust to a divorce. Both parents and children are strengthened by having shared and gone through a life crisis together.

PARENTING POINTERS

➤ In divorce, children need to be assured that they are not responsible for the problems between the parents.

➤ Children may regress or demonstrate negative behaviors in response to stress.

➤ Parents should initiate conversations with children about the divorce to help children air their feelings and concerns.

➤ Maintaining a positive relationship with the ex-spouse can help children with the adjustment to divorce.

62. Stepfamilies
Tolerance and understanding are keys to success

The blending of two families into one inevitably sparks conflict as families learn each others' idiosyncrasies. When difficulties and conflicts arise, stepfamilies often are worried that they're doing something wrong or that they are not normal. But conflict is normal in all families. In stepfamilies with usually at least one divorce in the background, members often feel reluctant to express any dissatisfaction because they may fear it will lead to another divorce. This makes it critical for stepfamilies to encourage communication.

Confronting conflict and learning to resolve problems is much better than trying to pretend conflict doesn't exist. Problems often escalate if ignored, therefore, family members need to learn ways to express themselves clearly and "fight fair." Parents and children should not become critical or accusatory. They should simply try to express how a situation makes them feel, and then discuss how to resolve it.

When a parent remarries, children typically experience several emotions, many of which are upsetting. They may feel responsible for the divorce. They may be disturbed that their routines have changed — sometimes with a new school, home, and friends. If there is joint custody or visitation, children may feel as if they live somewhere between households and are never completely in either one. All this may lead children to exhibit unusual behavior, such as emotional outbursts or unusual quietness.

These behavior changes are natural and to be expected. Like all trauma, it takes time for the emotional wounds caused by divorce to heal, and the healing process may not be complete by the time of the remarriage. Both parents and stepparents need to be tolerant, understanding, and observant. They should reassure children that they are not to blame for the divorce. Parents should tell children that they will always be loved and a valuable member of the family.

Even more importantly, parents need to understand the loyalty conflict that the child may be feeling. Initially kids may like their parent's interest in a new adult. But if the interest leads to marriage, no matter how wonderful the stepparent may be, he or she may be rejected. It's the rare exception for a stepparent to gain immediate acceptance. The child may feel as though the stepparent is trying to take the place of the other parent.

Often children just want to put their family back together the way it was. This fantasy is common among young children of divorce. Stepparents should try not to take the child's dislike of the new partner personally. It's often the situation, not the person, that the kid dislikes. A stepparent's role is to be another adult who is interested in this child — a caring person who may assume parental responsibilities and activities, but who will never be the actual parent.

It takes time for children to develop genuine loving feelings toward the stepparent. It's nice to be accepted and loved by a stepchild, but it may be asking for too much, especially at first. It helps for stepparents to mention, at times, the absent parent to make the stepchild understand that the stepparent knows how important the parent is in his life.

New stepparents often wonder if they belong in the family. They may see the closeness that existed between spouse and stepchildren in the single-parent family, and they wonder if they are intruding. They are often the target of much hostility from the children and they are unsure what role to take. They may feel overwhelmed by the stress, neglected by the new spouse, and disillusioned with the whole family.

Often, parents who remarry aren't prepared for the problems that emerge when they become a stepfamily. Since the new family system is trying to combine two families, each with its own history and style, confusing and conflicting feelings may occur. Parents can prepare themselves by reading as much as they can about stepfamilies and seeking professional counseling for the family if needed.

It's essential that stepfamilies realize that they are not alone in their struggles. Talking with others who have successfully formed stepfamilies in informal situations or support groups can help. Most important, avoid getting discouraged and giving up. With clear thinking, careful management, and patience, problems can be worked through, and a new stepfamily can become a close, caring unit.

PARENTING POINTERS

➤ Conflict in all families, including stepfamilies, is normal. Parents should encourage family members to discuss problems, rather than avoid them.

➤ Parents should understand that children will likely be upset by the many changes that they must endure through a remarriage, and that behavior problems can result.

➤ Parents should not push children to immediately embrace a new stepparent. However, in time, children can grow to accept and respect the new partner.

➤ Stepfamilies can get support by seeking out other stepfamilies and professional counseling, if necessary.

63. Family alcoholism
Helping children cope

Family alcoholism takes a heavy toll, especially on children. They are most vulnerable to the complex stresses that exist within an alcoholic family. Yet, because alcoholism is a family illness, all members are affected in varying degrees and in different ways. While this is a major issue to confront, there are some ways families can begin to cope with this difficult situation.

As with other family problems, young children may feel that they are responsible for an alcoholic parent's behavior. They believe that their actions can make the parent start or stop drinking. To correct this misperception, parents should discuss the disease of alcoholism with their children. If the parent is a recovering alcoholic, he or she could talk with the children directly. However, if that is not the case, others in the family still need to face the issue head on and explain the situation to the children. Understanding the disease may diminish children's feelings of guilt and blame. They need to know that no one chooses to be addicted to alcohol and that addiction happens. Children can't cause it, and they can't cure it any more than they could if the disease were cancer.

Children need predictability and a safe environment, yet parental addiction to alcohol brings unpredictable behavior that often causes an unsafe environment. Since denial is a significant factor in alcoholic families, these unpredictable behaviors and the resulting unhealthy situation for the children may be ignored. It's common to have a lack of communication in an alcoholic home. This inability to express feelings is a behavior that is learned by most children of alcoholics; this gives them a distorted sense of normal family life. Alcoholic families often try to disguise the situation as "not feeling well" or "under the weather" or "social drinking" when, in fact, there's a real illness that needs to be treated.

With continued denial this disease reaches beyond the generations with cycles of alcoholism that often are difficult to break. Two-thirds of adult alcoholics come from families with an alcoholic parent. Sixty percent of children of alcoholics are more likely to marry alcoholics. Experts estimate that 12-15 million school-age children live in alcoholic homes.

This cycle can end, however, when the family stops denying the problem, recognizes what is happening, and begins to work together toward recovery and healing. Once the alcoholic parent is in recovery and takes responsibility and owns the problem, he or she becomes a part of the healing process. Of course, recovery is a life-long process as different levels of self-understanding are reached.

Recovery is a difficult process that is different for everyone, with many ups and downs. During the recovery process negative patterns of family behavior need to be replaced with positive, nurturing ways of relating to each other. The alcoholic family certainly puts a great deal of energy into controlling or stopping the drinking, yet this energy can be channeled into new and healthy behaviors, such as family projects and time together to talk honestly and share experiences. Since alcoholic families tend to be private and somewhat reclusive, they can also benefit from networking with other families and being truthful with one another and their support system of friends and relatives.

New approaches to parenting are needed to prevent the cycle of family alcoholism from continuing. Parents in alcoholic families need to look at their patterns of child rearing and identify problem areas. For example, if lack of communication is a problem, parents can make a concerted effort to talk more with each other and with their kids. Parents and children can then recover and grow together using new and healthier approaches.

PARENTING POINTERS

➤ Children need to know the facts about alcoholism so they don't blame themselves for their parents' behavior.

➤ Alcoholic families often are in denial about the situation, which can lead to a lack of communication.

➤ When the alcoholic parent "owns" the problem, he becomes part of the joint healing process, which involves new and healthier patterns of behavior with frequent and truthful communication.

➤ Parents in alcoholic families should examine their parenting skills to identify problem areas that need to be addressed, and whether they are repeating parenting styles learned in their families of origin.

Summary

No one can be certain what new challenges and obstacles the future holds for families. Advances in technology, various media, and daily living promise to make life better. Yet, despite modern conveniences, our fast-paced lifestyle often comes with greater stressors, time-constraints, and quality of life issues.

Successful families now and in the future will need to continue working toward achieving a harmonious and peaceful existence in the home. Ongoing efforts and teamwork will go a long way to helping families meet their goals and enjoy a satisfying and rewarding life together.

Using this book as a reference, implementing its tips and guidelines, will help address most concerns as we enter the 21st century. Parents need to remember, however, that not every strategy works all the time and that people — parents and children — change over time.

The responsibility for maintaining a healthy, happy family rests with the parents, but as this book points out, children have a say in things too. By collaborating, cooperating, and at times compromising, parents and children can create an atmosphere of love, respect, and understanding — the foundation of a peaceful home.

Subject Index